W0009569

Published in U.S.A.
ISBN: 978-0-578-99972-2
Book design by Chad Spader

Visit www.thetogetherpress.com for more information.

THE TOGETHER PROJECT MANAGER

MAIA HEYCK-MERLIN

Table of Contents

Praise for *The Together Project Manager*

"The world does not lack for good ideas that could change the world, nor does the world lack for well intentioned, hardworking people who would genuinely like to see change happen. But what we do lack for far too often is enough people with the skill, tools, and confidence to translate their good ideas into action. Using her wealth of social sector experience, ever engaging style and superpower for planning everything from conferences for thousands to Girl Scout troop gatherings, Maia's the Together Project Manager provides us mere mortals with an easy to use step-by-step guide to successfully manage any project with the same grace, confidence and success that has been the hallmark of Maia's effectiveness over the years."
Jon Schwartz, COO/CFO, College Possible

"FINALLY—a book designed for Project Managers in education! The tools in The Together Project Manager can all be applied to the projects that I work on in my industry and I truly feel like I could apply any of them to my next project. As a longtime fan of *The Together Leader* and the tools associated with it, I was so excited to see some of the same tools and strategies referenced and applied to the context of project management. Thank you for making me excited to revisit and fine-tune my approach for my next project!" **Ashley Kogutkiewicz,** Project Manager, Charlotte-Mecklenburg Schools

"Maia's project management concepts and templates are so much more accessible than other more formal tools and trainings. Complex projects come with a dose of change, and I love the emphasis on communication, change management and real empathy for stakeholders rather than only tasks and deadlines. Maia knows it's all about the people, and she elevates the project manager to "leader"—you'll find just as many tips for engaging, surfacing tensions, aligning and celebrating as you will for tips on tracking to-do's. As usual, Maia's humor and relatability shine through and make this such a fun read, whether for first time project managers or experienced folks who need a refresher." **Genna Weinstein,** Director of People Operations, FullStory

"When you wake up and realize that you are tired of constantly building the ship as it is sailing, that's when you turn to Maia Heyck-Merlin's *The Together Project Manager.* Maia is well-versed in guiding educators and leaders through planning and time-management. In *The Together Project Manager,* Maia crafts the art of project management through a holistic approach which combines a balanced investment in the why and how. In addition, Maia's approach gives you the "bones" of project management, while incorporating all supporting systems (i.e., human capital, messaging, leadership, and more) to bring your project to life. This book highlights her ability to help us all keep it Together (pun intended) and effectively lead small and large-scale projects." **Daniel K. McKeown**, Director of Operations, Meeting Street Elementary, Charleston County School District

How to Access Your Templates and Resources

You now have access to a set of resources to help you act on the ideas in this book. Additionally, you can find modifiable templates based on the Together Tools referenced in each section.

To access templates for the tools we discuss throughout, please go to http://thetogetherpress.com/the-together-project-manager and enter the password: **saturdaytutoringprogram**

There you will find:

- **Templates:** In this folder you will find our Together Project Manager templates so that you can immediately put into practice what you've learned in this book.
- **Samples:** Here, you'll find all of the samples featured in the book.

Introduction

Why this book, and what do we mean by Project?!

There are a LOT of books out there about project management, but so many of them focus on technical aspects or just simply writing a plan. In our years of working with outstanding project managers in schools, districts and nonprofit organizations, The Together Group has seen the plan be ONE important piece of the overall process, but we have seen equally as much effort put into investment, motivation, and communication. In mission-driven work, our projects are anchored in deep meaning for Participants, recipients, and our communities. Whether you're building a new soccer field behind a school, overhauling a grant reporting system, or planning a team holiday party, our projects hold a deeper meaning than just the nuts and bolts of the results.

This book focuses on the entire cycle of project management, from start to finish, so you can kick off your project with confidence and close with competence. While we'll follow the basic tenets of excellent project management, we'll also help you invest people in the why, celebrate their contributions, and acknowledge how much of our work is tremendously important to other peoples' lives. As one of my trusted early readers put it, "Project work is people work." It's far too easy to create a pretty plan and start executing it, but lose sight of the outcome, unintentionally demotivate your team, and forget to adjust things along the way. But that's why you are here, right?

Let's start with defining what we ACTUALLY mean by "project."

WHAT IS A PROJECT, ANYWAY?

For our purposes, a project is anything in your work (or heck, personal!) life that:

- Has a distinct start and end
- Possesses a clear goal and purpose
- Contains many steps
- Involves multiple Participants
- Is possibly complex in nature

WHO NEEDS THIS BOOK

After training multiple people in our Together Project Manager courses over the past 15 years, we think virtually anyone can find this book useful! Most of our work focuses on nonprofits, schools, and other mission-driven entities, but you can apply our process to projects as varied as:

- Rolling out new HR software across your nonprofit
- Organizing a fundraising gala

- Scheduling summer training for new teachers
- Revising website content for your organization
- Designing attendance incentives for a Saturday tutoring program
- Planning high school graduation ceremonies

Whether you are a teacher, manager, division leader, superintendent, principal, or director of operations, we can all agree that being part of a project with strong leadership, clear communication, connection to the mission, and investment in the outcome makes it all the more enjoyable.

Disclaimer: *This book is **not** for you if you came here to learn how to format pivot tables in Excel (find a good online tutorial!), you want the latest project management software upgrade, or you're working independently on revamping your personal filing systems.*

So, what WILL we focus on? Coming up next!

WHO ARE WE?

Almost ten years ago, I released my first book, *The Together Teacher: Get Organized, Plan Ahead and Save Time.* I started training and supporting teachers who were sinking under the workload required, and soon expanded The Together Group to include trainings for Leaders, Team Members, and of course: Project Managers! Ten years and a global pandemic later, The Together Team now includes both online and in-person workshops. We hear constantly from Project Managers that they are drowning in way too many To-Dos and that they struggle to plan in advance, maintain flexibility, and support others in moving important work forward. And that's why the small but mighty Together Team has created this resource: to support you in planning, launching, and reflecting upon projects in a way that feels manageable and even joyful!

BELIEFS AND SKILLS OF A TOGETHER PROJECT MANAGER

We can create the most perfectly beautiful project management tools in the world, but they will only ever be as strong as the mindsets with which we back them up. After delivering Together Project Manager trainings online and in person for hundreds of partipants, we have identified key values to cultivate as we operate with our Together Tools.

Sound good? We will help you get there!

HOW TO USE THIS BOOK

We recommend reading this book start to finish in one shot with an actual project in mind. This will work best if it's a project you have yet to start, but you anticipate will be complex and spread across multiple teams. You may also find it beneficial to read this book with your team, and then decide if there are any practices you would like to implement together. We have found that project planning language is most beneficial when used consistently across a group of people, more so than any of our Together Tools.

While reading this book the first time, please be reflection ready (have a notebook / writing tool /blank document on hand!) and keep the Together Templates open on your digital device. This book is designed to be read—with your own project in hand—in a quick sitting or two. By keeping chapters short, reflection exercises ready, and examples easy-to-follow, our hope is that you can pick and choose which project learnings will benefit your work the most—and immediately apply them. There are a few handy-dandy learning tools we want to highlight.

The Most Together Project Managers:

- Deeply understand the goal of the project, why it is important, and to whom else it is important

- Feel strong ownership over the outcomes of the project

- Clearly articulate project expectations so all Project Participants are clear on roles

- Plan ahead thoughtfully, understand how all the pieces fit together, and have strong command of the details

- Motivate others to make decisions, suggest recommendations, and get the work done

- Get people excited about the project's impact and showcase successes along the way

- Proactively identify stumbling blocks, pitfalls, and other possible project detours

- Communicate predictably about project progress along the way

- Respond nimbly to changes in plan, both expected and unexpected

- Celebrate, codify, and close the project with grace

Re-read the previous statements and consider your last project. Rate yourself on a quick scale of "always, sometimes, rarely, never."

When have you exhibited your best Together Project Manager skills? What kinds of environments supported this? Where do you need to grow?

Reader Reflection Questions: At the end of each tool or topic, you will find reflection questions or exercises to apply to your own project. If it is helpful to see all Reader Reflections in one place, you can print them here or view them at thetogetherpress.com/the-together-project-manager.

Together Tearaway: If you prefer a shorter takeaway section, take a peek at our Together Tearaway on page 127, designed to be torn (quite literally) out of the back of the hard copy. If you are reading the digital version, you can print a version over at thetogetherpress.com/the-together-project-manager.

Together Templates: Throughout each chapter, you will see reference to modifiable Together Project Manager tools. We don't anticipate you will need all of our Templates; some of that depends on the complexity of your project. You can download these from thetogetherpress.com/the-together-project-manager and use them as a starter kit for your own tools.

HOW THIS BOOK IS ORGANIZED

We'll follow ONE example throughout this entire book: Kelly, a fictional member of a fictional central office in a fictional large school district, has been tasked with starting a fictional Saturday tutoring program. Kelly's work will model each aspect of the project planning process. You'll apply your learnings to your own project as we go, too!

Kelly's Tutoring Program

Kelly, a leader on a student support team within a school district's central office, has been asked to start a Saturday tutoring program for students across the district. This will be a new initiative for the district, and district leaders are very excited about the program. The details Kelly gets when she's asked to lead the project include:

- **The why:** Extra academic support is a key component of students' academic success.
- **The what:** The tutoring program is meant to boost academic results for students who are most struggling to meet their academic goals.
- **The when:** It's currently mid-summer, and the program needs to start in January.
- **The who:** Kelly will need to build a Project Team with representatives from the Teaching & Learning, Finance, Facilities, and Data & Analytics teams. Kelly will also have the support of her manager, Frank. Additionally, she will need to engage, invest, and communicate with Stakeholders across multiple school sites, including principals, teachers, parents, and students.

LET'S DO THIS!

Becoming a Together Project Manager does not follow a straight line, and while there is a process to heed, your project may require different steps, unique sequencing, or additional information. That's cool, only you know your project best! We trust you are here to enhance your own skills and only take up our offerings as you need them. As you have revelations and celebrations, please share them with us on social media with a **#togetherprojectmanager**.

 **Instagram:**
@together_teacher

 **Facebook:**
facebook.com/thetogetherteacher

To keep us all anchored in the same flow, we'll use the graphic on the next page to organize ourselves as we work through the sections of this book.

You may find need a different order, or that not all of the deliverables are necessary, or that you want to skip steps along the way. Let me repeat myself—that's JUST FINE! As you start new projects in the future, you can use this outline to lead with confidence. At the end of this book, we want you to be able to say, "I'm the kind of Together Project Manager who plans in advance, practices flexibility when things change, invests people in the purpose, supports my team in getting the work done, communicates strategically, and celebrates completion." Bam!

Throughout each chapter, you'll also find FAQs, definitions, templates, and Reader Reflections to help you think about your project.

What is your project? Why does it matter to your organization?

Let's start with getting our project primed and ready to go!

What do you want your Project Team to say about what it's like to work with you on a project?

	CHAPTER OBJECTIVES	TOGETHER TOOL
1. **Prime the Project**	• Ask yourself useful Project Pre-Work Questions • Draft a Project Statement to align with your Participants • Write a Project Summary to finalize the project	✔ Project Statement ✔ Project Summary
2. **Create Clear Project Roles & Responsibilities**	• Get clear about the actual project work that needs to be done • Figure out who is best positioned to take on which tasks • Determine how to communicate about the project work with your Participants	✔ Clear Roles and Responsibilities ✔ Project Job Description
3. **Plan the Project**	• Determine which Project Planning tool is most effective for you • Decide which Project Columns are necessary for your project • Create Project Buckets to begin chronological project thinking • Break down Project Buckets into Project Tasks	✔ Project Plan
4. **Launch the Project**	• Differentiate your project communication for various Project Stakeholders • Determine your method for launching your project into the world	✔ Project Communications Chart ✔ Project Launch Agenda ✔ Project Launch Emails
5. **Manage Yourself & Others**	• Conduct a Weekly Project Review to keep tasks and the Project Team on track • Create and protect time to do your own Project Work • Design and implement Project Meetings and various forms of communication	✔ Weekly Project Reviews ✔ Project Meeting Agendas
6. **Close & Codify the Project**	• Gather ongoing data to help inform outcomes • Facilitate a Project Debrief to consider successes and challenges • Codify learnings for the future	✔ Formal and Informal Project Feedback ✔ Project Debrief ✔ Project Codification Plan

	CHAPTER OBJECTIVES	TOGETHER TOOL
1. **Prime the Project**	• Ask yourself useful Project Pre-Work Questions • Draft a Project Statement to align with your Participants • Write a Project Summary to finalize the project	✔ Project Statement ✔ Project Summary
2. **Create Clear Project Roles & Responsibilities**	• Get clear about the actual project work that needs to be done • Figure out who is best positioned to take on which tasks • Determine how to communicate about the project work with your Participants	✔ Clear Roles and Responsibilities ✔ Project Job Description
3. **Plan the Project**	• Determine which Project Planning tool is most effective for you • Decide which Project Columns are necessary for your project • Create Project Buckets to begin chronological project thinking • Break down Project Buckets into Project Tasks	✔ Project Plan
4. **Launch the Project**	• Differentiate your project communication for various Project Stakeholders • Determine your method for launching your project into the world	✔ Project Communications Chart ✔ Project Launch Agenda ✔ Project Launch Emails
5. **Manage Yourself & Others**	• Conduct a Weekly Project Review to keep tasks and the Project Team on track • Create and protect time to do your own Project Work • Design and implement Project Meetings and various forms of communication	✔ Weekly Project Reviews ✔ Project Meeting Agendas
6. **Close & Codify the Project**	• Gather ongoing data to help inform outcomes • Facilitate a Project Debrief to consider successes and challenges • Codify learnings for the future	✔ Formal and Informal Project Feedback ✔ Project Debrief ✔ Project Codification Plan

1

PRIME THE PROJECT— aka Get the Project Pre-Work in Order

In this chapter, you will learn to:
- Ask yourself useful Project Pre-Work Questions
- Draft a Project Statement to align with your Participants
- Write a Project Summary to finalize the project

While the instinct to immediately jump into the work is understandable, we first need to make sure your project is properly primed. If you start by frantically listing all of your To-Dos into a Google Sheet without considering the project's overall purpose, the people involved, and your ideal outcome, you could end up just following a checklist that doesn't achieve the results you want. Let's say you were tasked, like Kelly, with creating a Saturday tutoring program. If you dive right into researching curriculum offerings, updating student enrollment software, and writing tutor job descriptions, you risk running into Checking Boxes Only (let's call it CBO!) without understanding what you hope to really achieve. This may leave you unable to pivot, step back, and communicate.

Let's get this project primed!

This chapter will lead us through Project Pre-work, and then move to Project Statements and Summaries., While I know we are excited to just jump in, we can assure you that having done this heavy lifting in advance will prevent project bumps later. Let's get into our Project Pre-Work—which will help us ultimately communicate and plan with others later.

KELLY'S TUTORING PROGRAM: PROJECT PRE-WORK

Kelly, mentioned in the introduction, has a project dropped in her lap during the summer: Create a Saturday Tutoring Program to launch in the spring semester to provide extra support for students in foundational skills. Before Kelly researches curriculum options, we want her to step back and summarize her understanding of the project first. This is to ensure she has a full grasp of what she's taking on, what she already knows, what will be required of her as she moves forward.

Kelly drafts a list of questions about the tutoring program focused on the following buckets: Outcome and goals, Participants, decision-makers, deliverables, timeline, and budget. Let's look at her brain dump by bucket.

Draft a list of questions you need to ask about your project. Use the buckets listed previously to help jog your thinking.

Topics	General Questions	Additional Questions for Kelly's Tutoring Project
Rationale	Why do we need this project? How does this project reflect our mission, vision, and goals?	How does this program align to and support our academic strategy?
Vision	What does success look like? What are the key deliverables? Are there any pre-established goals?	What impact on academic growth do we hope to see? How many students are we trying to reach? What's the anticipated longevity of this program? Is it one-year-only? Or a pilot program that might be expanded in future years?
Process	What is the level of priority to the organization? Who are the Stakeholders? What do they know already? Who are the decision-makers? What's our overall timeline? What are the major deadlines? Are there must-do's? Things to avoid-at-all-costs? Are there other projects' deadlines we need to align to?	Has anything similar been done in the district before? Or nearby districts? If yes, what do we want to replicate or change? Who has expressed interest in the tutoring program? Are we responding to "demand" for the program, or will we need to create it? Who is going to have strong opinions about this project?
Resources	What is my budget? Who can help me? What are other existing resources, e.g. documents, data?	For the project team: who should I work with from Teaching & Learning, Finance, Facilities, and Data & Analytics teams?

1.1 Kelly's List of Questions

DRAFT AND RESEARCH POSSIBLE ANSWERS TO YOUR PROJECT PRE-WORK

And because we don't believe that asking a lot of open-ended questions to very busy people gets us very far, Kelly will take the step of drafting ANSWERS to her questions as well. Even if she doesn't have much of a starting point, she knows it is her job as the project lead to figure it out. Worst case scenario is that she guessed wrong!

Now that we have these questions laid out in the buckets previously, let's think about how to answer them. Kelly reviews her full list of questions and thinks through what she can answer herself. She then prioritizes the other questions she needs help answering, and picks a handful of top priority questions to discuss with her manager at their next meeting. Kelly even takes the step to draft an email to her manager in advance of the upcoming meeting.

Because getting clear on these questions is critical to her own path forward, Kelly drafts an email to her manager in preparation for an upcoming one-on-one meeting. Kelly is going to take the step of also drafting answers to her questions—knowing that this will advance the conversation faster. Let's peek at her model.

What if I don't know the answers to draft my project pre-work?

We get it. We have been there. But, but, but, these answers are not going to magically fall in our laps, so we have to go after them.

From:	Kathleen		
To:	Frank		Cc Bcc
Subject:	**Saturday Tutoring Project – questions (and draft answers) for ...**		Priority ∨

Calibri (Body) ∨ 11 ∨ A ∨ **B** *I* U ab 🖉 ∨ x² x₂ ≣ ≣ ≡ ∨ ⤒ ⤓ ∘∘∘

Hi Frank,

I'm excited to dig into the new Saturday Tutoring Program! To help me get started, I've got a few high-priority questions I'm hoping to answer so that I can get started.

Let's plan on talking through these in our next check-in; in the meantime, I've tried drafting answers to these questions to give us a starting point.

My question	Drafted answer—to review and confirm or revise with you
What does success look like?	Some measure of academic outcomes Enrollment: strong participation across campuses, recruitment of students who need tutoring support the most Strong project planning and execution, including stakeholder engagement and communication
What are the key deliverables?	Communications Plan Budget Decision about which curriculum to use Something around tutoring hiring and training?
For the project team: who should I work with from Teaching & Learning, Finance, Facilities, and Data & Analytics teams?	Teaching and Learning: Pablo Finance: Tonya Facilities: Helen or Dylan? Data and Analytics: the new Assistant Director of Data and Analytics they are hiring?
Are there must-dos? Things to avoid-at-all-costs?	We need to intentionally research and select a curriculum. Some of our schools already use a tutoring curriculum, and this is an opportunity to align around one to use district-wide We know principals have felt left out of planning for district-wide initiatives like this in the past; we must be intentional about engaging them throughout the planning and execution process

I'll definitely have more questions as I work through preparing to launch this project :-)
But talking through these soon will be a helpful first step!

Best,

Kelly

1.2 Kelly's Project Questions and Draft Answers

The question and answer work you just completed will help you drive towards the next step of your planning process. Now that we have all of our questions noted and a path established to get some of our answers, we are ready to move into our first official planning document: The Project Statement. You can think about your Statement as the 30,000 foot view of your work.

DRAFT A PROJECT STATEMENT

The reason to design a Statement before getting started is to confirm:

- Is the purpose of your project super clear to all involved?
- Are all people involved in your project aware of one another?
- Are Participants and other Stakeholders motivated by the impact of your project?
- Have you laid out a simple timeline for your project?

Kelly needs to create a Statement to share with her manager, colleagues, and other people who will assist with her tutoring program. Kelly can bring her Statement to various meetings to invest others, seek input on outcomes, and identify any hurdles on the front end. She can use the information from her Project Pre-Work to create her Project Statement.

Project Statement: A one-page summary, often including snazzy visuals, that articulates the purpose, Participants, and timeline of your project. It is created to introduce others to the project's main goal, available resources, and timeline. Or, more simply stated: Purpose, Participants, Phases. The Project Statement will be used during initial project meetings or introductions to secure help from others and to get everyone on the same page at the outset of the project.

Kelly's Tutoring Program

For her Statement, Kelly will build one clear slide that shows the:

- **Purpose of her Project:** Extra academic support is a key component of student success
- **Participants in her Project:** Principals, tutors, various departments.
- **Phases of her Project:** Thoughtful consideration of upfront input, logistics, curriculum, and training.

Kelly can bring her Project Statement to various meetings to invest others, seek input on outcomes, and identify any hurdles on the front end.

PROJECT MANAGER | **STATEMENT**

Project Title: Saturday Tutoring Program
Our "Why": Extra academic support is a key component of students' academic success
Big Goal: 100% of participating students will meet their individual academic growth goals

	August	September	October
Project Phase	Partner with principals to direction-set and build investment	Plan logistics: curriculum, hiring, budgeting, facilities	Recruit tutors and students
Participants (Project Team & ...)	Principals, District Leadership	Principals, Teaching & Learning, Facilities, Finance	Principals, Human Resources

1.3: Kelly's Tutoring Program Project Statement

Now, back to work on YOUR Project Statement, shall we?

Time Commitment: You will need 60–120 minutes to create your Project Statement. It can be easy to get caught up in formatting, so we recommend sketching out the content first. I know, I know, it can feel overwhelming to spend this much time up front, but we promise it will pay you back. When you make the effort now to rally people around purpose, secure commitments from Participants, and align on timeline, you'll really reduce future pauses, detours, and communication mishaps. Identify as many predictable events as you can now!

PROJECT MANAGER	STATEMENT					⏱

Project Title: _____
Our "Why": _____
Big Goal: _____

	Month	Month	Month	Month	Month	Month
Project Phase						
Participants						

RESOURCES: template

1.4: Project Statement Template

Build your Project Statement. If you don't want to start from scratch, definitely download one of our starter templates from thetogetherpress.com/the-together-project-manager.

After you create your Project Statement, you'll want to shop it around to your various Stakeholders. Start with getting sign-off from your manager and then see who else is impacted. Typically, the Statement is used for the most senior members of the organization (picture a CEO or Superintendent) flipping through a binder of all of the projects currently running, and now we need to get more detailed for the people actually involved in the day-to-day work of the project. Remember—any chance you have now to talk about your project is a way to get people motivated around your mission!

Now that we are aligned on big picture, let's dig in a little deeper. Enter The Project Summary! And if you are itching to get started on that Project Plan now, hold your horses, it is coming. But doing this project priming is going to make writing the Project Plan super easy, we promise!

CREATE A PROJECT SUMMARY

Now that the Project Statement has been used to confirm alignment on purpose, Participants, and phases, it's time to go into a bit more detail. We need to build out a Project Summary.

What if there is significant pushback after I share my Statement?

This can definitely happen. If it does, aren't you glad you caught wind of this tension sooner rather than later? We recommend figuring out the reason for the pushback. Is it budget? Timeline? Purpose? Sometimes the entire project can actually get scrapped at this stage. Perhaps your team, division, or manager wants the project to proceed but others don't. Don't get discouraged if your project doesn't immediately get the green light! The point of this pre-work is to tease these issues out early in the project game.

FAQ

> **Project Summary:** A 1–2 page overview of your project, outlining the intended outcomes, key deadlines, roles and responsibilities, and budget for your project. It is often shared with the actual Project Team so they can see the big picture before they sign on. The audience for your Summary is typically the actual project Participants, the people involved in the day-to-day work and decision-making of your project. Let's return to Kelly's Tutoring Program.

Kelly's Tutoring Program

Now that Kelly has gained investment using her Statement, she is ready to think about her project with one more level of detail. She needs to write her Project Summary, which she will use to share with the various people who will help her with the tutoring program—the curriculum team, the facilities point person, the school building points of contact, and the HR team who oversees hiring. It is critical each of these individuals and teams understands where they fit into the bigger picture of the process. If they do not understand their roles, they may make decisions in isolation that don't support the project's outcomes or not feel as invested in the overall project goals.

As you can see in Kelly's Project Summary, she has a few components in place:

- She gave her project a name and a motto.
  We love making projects fun!
- Project goals and criteria for success are crystal clear
- Project roles are explained clearly for all involved
  (more on this in the next chapter!)
- Deliverables, budget, and project stages
  are planned ahead

Create your own Project Summary. If you find our templates helpful, you can locate them here thetogetherpress.com/the-together-project-manager. If you already know answers to all of your questions, this will take you about an hour to complete. If you have to go back to your Project Pre-Work, this process may take a few hours.

The Project Summary is important because, just like the Project Statement, if you catch issues with any phase of the project now, you can resolve them up front. When it is actual Project Plan time, you will sail some smooth project seas. Okay, I took that one too far.

Kelly will set individual meetings with each member of the Project Team to review their roles in the project and tell them what to expect and when. For some meetings, Kelly will share her Statement or Summary in advance. In other cases, she will review the project with the individuals verbally and follow up afterward with the Summary. How to decide what info to share formally in advance, present in the moment, or follow up with after? It really depends on the Project Personalities (couldn't resist that bit of alliteration!). For example,

Review Your Project Summary. Check your work against Kelly's criteria:

- ❑ Project is named and clearly defined
- ❑ Goals and success are crystal clear
- ❑ Project roles are clearly explained for all involved
- ❑ Deliverables, budget and project stages are planned ahead

when working with a colleague who is a very detailed planner and wants to know everything up front, you may want to consider sharing more information ahead of time. For the more casual project participant, it may work better to share your Summary in the moment and then follow up with a recap. The point here is to carefully consider each person's style and differentiate your approach accordingly.

 **SUMMARY**

Project Name: Saturday Tutoring Program

Project Motto: Team Work Makes the Dream Work ⬅————— **Project Motto**

Project Definition: Create and execute the logistics, budget, curriculum, communication and evaluation plan for a replicable Saturday tutoring plan for one DOE district (23 schools).

Project Goals ⬅————————— **Project Goals**

- **Big Goal**
  - o 100% of students meet their individual academic growth goals (growth goal to be determined with principal and teacher input)
- **Process Goals**
  - o Select clear and accessible curriculum that will lead to significant student achievement gains
  - o Determine and execute the logistics such that tutoring starts/ends on time, facilities are clean and ready for tutoring, everyone has the materials they need, and all instructional time is spent on instruction and not on operational concerns
  - o Communicate with stakeholders (namely principals, tutors and students) such that we identify the highest-need students, set clear outcomes for their growth, and tutor/student attendance is 97%/95% per Saturday respectively
  - o Tutoring is delivered and executed at or under budget.

Project Team Members & Roles ⬅————— **Project Roles**

- **Kelly,** *Assistant Director of Student Support* – Project Lead
- **Frank,** *Managing Director of Student Support* – Project Sponsor
- **Helen,** *Facilities Director* – Lead planning and execution for facilities
- **Pablo,** *Assistant Director of Teaching and Learning* – Manage curriculum selection and lead tutor training
- **Tonya,** *Manager of Student Support Finances* – Manage budget and provide financial oversight
- **Dante,** *Assistant Director of Data and Analytics* – Manage evaluation of student achievement results

Key Project Deliverables ⬅————— **Deliverables**

- Communication Plan
- Budget
- Curriculum
- Facilities plan (where and when)
- Tutor Training: scope & sequence and execution

RESOURCES: template

1.5A: Kelly's Project Summary

Project Budget ←

- Facilities: $6,100
- Tutoring: $128,000
- Curriculum: $4,900
- Materials: $1,900
- Training: $9,100

Budget & Stages/ Schedule

Main Project Phases

August	September	October	November	December	January – End of Year
Principal engagement (program design)				Principal communication (progress updates)	
Logistical planning (budget, facilities)					
Curriculum selection					
		Tutor hiring		Tutor training	
		Student recruitment			
					Logistical Execution & Course-Correction
					Evaluation

1.5B: Kelly's Project Summary

Project Name: _____

Project Motto: _____

Project Definition: _____

Project Goals

- **Big Goals**
  - X
  - Y
  - Z
- **Process Goals**
  - X
  - Y
  - Z

Project Team Members & Roles

- **Name A** – Role
- **Name B** – Role
- **Name C** – Role

Key Project Deliverables

- Deliverable 1
- Deliverable 2
- Deliverable 3

Project Budget

- $X
- $Y
- $Z

Main Project Phases

Month 1	Month 2	Month 3	Month 4	Month 5	Month 6

RESOURCES: template

1.6: Project Summary Template

The Together Project Manager

What if my project is controversial, tricky, or charged with political tripwires?

Excellent question! And a good one to be aware of now. Consider what Pre-Project work you can do to assess levels of investment, individual worries, and so on. Here are a few ways to pull this off:

1. **Schedule individual meetings to verbally explain the project and suss out concerns and motivations.** You can then build these worries into your Statement or Summary.

2. **Conduct a Pre-Project Survey to assess opinions on various aspects of the project.** This can come in handy when you launch your project and can say things like, "85% of our principals agree this program is necessary."

3. **Ask who else has an interest in this project.** Use your emotional and organizational intelligence to put out feelers for people who are curious, skeptical, or somewhere in between, and get creative about including them in your design and roll-out processes.

Let's put this all together, shall we? We think about Plans in three overall phases. The simplest is the Statement, then we get more details in the Summary, and finally, we blow out all the details in the actual Project Plan. We just hit the first two, and we will roll into the actual detailed every-day-sortable Project Plan in our next chapter.

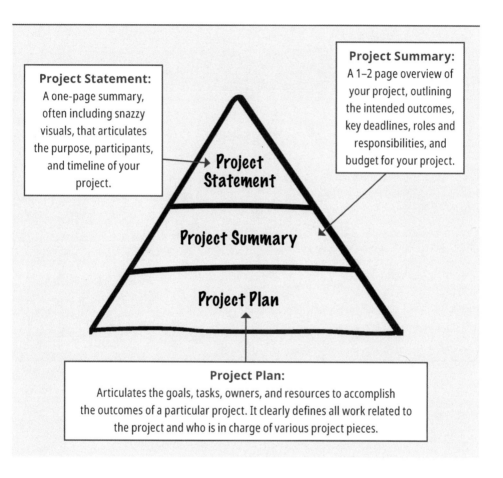

Okay, this is good. We are making progress. Now that we've built investment and motivation, we need to make sure we'll have the right help to take our Project to the finish line. Creating clear Roles and Responsibilities helps us make specific asks of others, AND get super clear on our own duties.

Who needs to see your Project Summary?
What is your plan to share it with them?

Who Needs to see your Summary?	How and When will you share?	What is the most important thing(s) you want this person to know about the project?

	CHAPTER OBJECTIVES	TOGETHER TOOL
1. **Prime the Project**	• Ask yourself useful Project Pre-Work Questions • Draft a Project Statement to align with your Participants • Write a Project Summary to finalize the project	✔ Project Statement ✔ Project Summary
2. **Create Clear Project Roles & Responsibilities**	• Get clear about the actual project work that needs to be done • Figure out who is best positioned to take on which tasks • Determine how to communicate about the project work with your Participants	✔ Clear Roles and Responsibilities ✔ Project Job Description
3. **Plan the Project**	• Determine which Project Planning tool is most effective for you • Decide which Project Columns are necessary for your project • Create Project Buckets to begin chronological project thinking • Break down Project Buckets into Project Tasks	✔ Project Plan
4. **Launch the Project**	• Differentiate your project communication for various Project Stakeholders • Determine your method for launching your project into the world	✔ Project Communications Chart ✔ Project Launch Agenda ✔ Project Launch Emails
5. **Manage Yourself & Others**	• Conduct a Weekly Project Review to keep tasks and the Project Team on track • Create and protect time to do your own Project Work • Design and implement Project Meetings and various forms of communication	✔ Weekly Project Reviews ✔ Project Meeting Agendas
6. **Close & Codify the Project**	• Gather ongoing data to help inform outcomes • Facilitate a Project Debrief to consider successes and challenges • Codify learnings for the future	✔ Formal and Informal Project Feedback ✔ Project Debrief ✔ Project Codification Plan

The Together Project Manager

2

CREATE CLEAR PROJECT ROLES AND RESPONSIBILITIES — Who Is Doing What?!

In this chapter, you will learn to:

- Get clear about the actual project work that needs to be done
- Figure out who is best positioned to take on which tasks
- Determine how to communicate about the project work with your Participants

The reason it is actually called a PROJECT is that you are not doing all of the work yourself! Rather, you are coordinating and collaborating with other people to accomplish a shared outcome. To keep your project humming, we have to be sure to make sure everyone knows their particular roles.

CREATE CLEAR ROLES AND RESPONSIBILITIES

The more specific we are when delegating tasks and assignments, the better the outcome will be overall. In this section, we are going to create a Roles and Responsibilities Chart so that we can be very clear about who is doing what within our project. This will allow others to plan ahead, understand their roles, and block time to contribute to the project. The easiest analogy that comes to mind is planning a potluck versus a specific holiday meal. Picture when you plan a specific holiday meal, you have a clearer vision of what you want; you may say, "Please bring an appetizer that can serve 12, and make sure to include serving utensils!" You also probably think about who has better baking skills, and that person gets assigned dessert. Someone with less gifts in the culinary department is told to bring some fresh bread! You are matching each person's strengths to their task. For your Project, think about which outcome you want and how specific you need to be.

WHO SHOULD TAKE ON THE PROJECT WORK

Kelly's Tutoring Program

Let's start by considering the following questions:

- **What is the actual work to be done?** Are you delegating an entire bucket of the project or just bite-sized tasks?
- **Who has certain areas of expertise or skill?** For example, in Kelly's Tutoring Program, she knows the budget work will need to be handled by a particular procurement person who knows how to code the purchases properly.
- **Who is primed in the right spot in the organization?** In the Tutoring Program, Kelly needs a strong instructional eye to determine which curriculum to use. This person will also need to be able to influence the principals.

- **Who is hungry for a stretch assignment?** Kelly knows that the CAO's assistant really wants to learn to interview people. Kelly is going to ask to pull her in for some of the tutor interviews to invest in her capacity. Yes, it will be more work to train her, but this will be a helpful skill for her to build in the long run.
- **Who has extra capacity at the moment?** *(stop laughing!)*
- **What could be outsourced to a third party, such as a vendor, intern, or consultant?**

As you consider who should take on various parts of the Project Work, you may get very excited and want to lock it all in immediately, but keep in mind that you will likely need to return to this after a few more of the planning details are in place. The point is to be intentional of people's roles from the beginning, rather than let the assignments happen by default. Go back to that holiday dinner party example. We want to be clear who is bringing the dinner rolls, why they received that assignment, and make sure it happens!

A lot of this depends on how primed the team is to take on the work, so let's start with how much prior knowledge people have about the project overall and how easily you can access them.

- **When assignments are crystal clear** You can simply hold a meeting or email folks to inform them of their duties.
- **When you have an idea of who should take on the work, but you don't have approval to ask them:** You can write a job description and then check with managers or other gatekeepers.
- **When there's less clarity about who can take on certain tasks or project buckets:** You may have to write a more detailed job description and shop it around your organization to see if there are any "takers."

Some of your organizations may have clear language for Participants in place, such as RACI or MOCHA. Not sure what those even mean? We got you! Check out the following Project Vocabulary, and if you need a more detailed explanation, head over to our Glossary at the end of the book.

RACI: A matrix that helps team members understand their role for each step in the Project Plan. For each item or task, it establishes who:

- is **Responsible**
- is **Accountable**
- needs to be **Consulted**
- should be **Informed**[1]

MOCHA: MOCHA is a similar acronym that helps team members understand who is responsible for each task:

- the **Manager**
- the **Owner**
- to be **Consulted**
- the **Helper**
- the **Approver**[2]

And if this all sounds like jibberish to you, let's pause. Think about a time when you were part of a project, and you were unclear on your own role. What happened? How did you feel? Consider the holiday dinner party earlier in the chapter. Did you dare just guess what the host wants at the table or did you want to know your actual expectations in advance? Without this kind of clarity, outcomes are not as strong, processes are bumpier than necessary, and personal frustration abounds. Sidebar: I'm all for a good potluck, but not when the stakes are high.

---

1. Developed by Kristoffer V. Grude, Tor Haug and Erling S. Andersen
2. Developed by The Management Center

Whether your organization has a working definition of project roles you can slide right into or you are introducing project language for the first time, let's try to get this right for the sake of you, your Participants, and your project!

Kelly's Tutoring Program

Kelly's project includes a lot of people with a lot of opinions. She uses MOCHA (see next page) to clarify who is doing what overall, and even for specific project buckets.

In some cases, the manager and approver may be the same person, as might the consulted and the helpers. Once you have a common language established, you may need to think about how to apply this to your actual project. In Kelly's case, she has a lot of Helpers. She will want to get super clear about what she wants and needs from each one, basically spelling out job descriptions.

Wait, what?! Project Job Descriptions?!

Yes, you heard me right. If you're going to sign on for a project, it is helpful to know what you are actually and truly responsible for, how much time it will take, and roughly when it will happen. Caveat: As with all aspects of this book, pick and choose only what will serve you. Sometimes, a Job Description may be unnecessary. This is especially true in smaller organizations where you can roll your chair right over to your colleague in the next cubicle and say, "Hey, I'm going to need some help on this project." But in larger organizations where there may be procedures for borrowing time from other teams, or established communication protocols, you may find you need to be more systematic.

Project Bucket	Manager	Owner	Consulted	Helpers	Approver
	Assigns responsibility and holds owner accountable. Makes suggestions, asks hard questions, reviews progress, serves as a resource, and intervenes if the work is off-track.	Has overall responsibility for the success or failure of the project. Ensures that all the work gets done (directly or with helpers) and that others are involved appropriately. There should only be one owner.	Should be asked for input or needs to be bought in to the project.reflect our mission, vision, and goals?	Assists with or does some of the work.	Signs off on decisions before they're final.
Overall	Frank	Kelly	Chief Academic Officer, Principal Managers, Principals, Teachers, Parents, Students	Tonya, Helen, Pablo, Dante	Superintendent
Principal Communication & Engagement	Frank	Kelly	Principal Managers	Principal Managers	Frank
Budget	Frank	Kelly	Helen, Pablo	Helen, Pablo	Tonya
Facilities	Kelly	Helen	Kelly, Principals	On-site facilities team	Helen's Manager

2.1 Kelly's MOCHA draft (continued on next page)

CREATE AN ACTUAL PROJECT JOB DESCRIPTION

I know, I know, you are READY to move on that Plan. We are so close, but we still need to get a little more specific with some of our project roles. This is important. Let's say we ask someone to help us with the project and they ask more about:

- What exactly am I responsible for?
- When are the deliverables due?
- What is the timeline for my involvement?

To get the help we need, we gotta be ready to answer!

Kelly's Tutoring Program

When shopping around her Project Summary, Kelly realized she needed to get incredibly clear on what her actual ask was of her teammates, both to secure commitments from their managers and also from the team members themselves. She got right down to exactly what she needed from the Academic Team, at a painstaking level of detail. Let's peek at a sample job description now.

Kelly spells out key responsibilities, specifies actual deliverables, and gets clear on required time commitment.

You may be starting to think, "Oh, my goodness, Maia! This is going to take me so much time!!!" Great point. You only need to go to this level of Job Description if:

- **It will be easier to secure Participants** if people are crystal clear on what's being asked of them
- You think the people joining your Project Team **need a better understanding of the work** involved
- **You've been leading portions** of the Project yourself and now **need to hand them off**
- You're **not quite sure of the workload yourself**, and writing job descriptions will help you gauge it

There may be times when you are not even sure what the actual work of the project will entail, so how on earth could you even consider writing a Project Job Description? Well, we think it is worth the time to attempt to write out the expectations so you can be clear what you are asking for. In some cases, let's say, of content or bucket area expertise, you may lack the technical chops to write a job description, but we encourage you to co-create it with whomever is helping.

Congratulations! Your Project is primed! You've created your Statement, written out your Summary, and designed clear Roles and Responsibilities—with detailed Project Job Descriptions (as needed) to match.

Now it's time to write your actual Plan! Finally! Let's dive in!

Do you need Project Job Descriptions? Which ones are easy to write? Which are more challenging? Take a pause to sketch out what your Project Job Descriptions need in them. If you need a starting point, check out our Together Templates at thetogetherpress. com/the-together-project-manager.

 | **JOB DESCRIPTION**

Project Name: Saturday Tutoring Program

Project Job Title: Instructional Lead

Owner of Role: Pablo (Assistant Director of Teaching and Learning)

Key Responsibilities

- Own the curriculum selection and procurement process:
    - Identify criteria for selecting curriculum (non-negotiables and nice-to-haves)
    - Research curriculum options and set up demos as necessary
    - Recommend a curriculum decision with a clear rationale
    - Purchase selected curriculum
    - Serve as main contact for questions about the curriculum throughout program execution
- Lead tutor training:
    - Develop a training scope and sequence
    - Develop lesson plans with clear objectives and multiple opportunities for practice and feedback
    - Plan and execute training logistics (scheduling, space, materials, technology, meals, etc.)
- Actively contribute to building a strong project team:
    - Attend project team launch call and bi-weekly project team meetings
    - Huddle with Kelly for 20 minutes 1x/week
    - Contribute to building the project plan; update the project plan at least 1x/week
    - Communicate proactively with all members of the project team
    - Give and receive feedback so that we all grow together

Key Deliverables

- Recommendation for a clear and accessible curriculum that will lead to significant student achievement gains
- Tutor training scope & sequence and lesson plans
- Tutor trainings in December (execution)

2.2 Kelly's Project Job Description for Pablo

	CHAPTER OBJECTIVES	TOGETHER TOOL
1. **Prime the Project**	• Ask yourself useful Project Pre-Work Questions • Draft a Project Statement to align with your Participants • Write a Project Summary to finalize the project	✔ Project Statement ✔ Project Summary
2. **Create Clear Project Roles & Responsibilities**	• Get clear about the actual project work that needs to be done • Figure out who is best positioned to take on which tasks • Determine how to communicate about the project work with your Participants	✔ Clear Roles and Responsibilities ✔ Project Job Description
3. **Plan the Project**	• Determine which Project Planning tool is most effective for you • Decide which Project Columns are necessary for your project • Create Project Buckets to begin chronological project thinking • Break down Project Buckets into Project Tasks	✔ Project Plan
4. **Launch the Project**	• Differentiate your project communication for various Project Stakeholders • Determine your method for launching your project into the world	✔ Project Communications Chart ✔ Project Launch Agenda ✔ Project Launch Emails
5. **Manage Yourself & Others**	• Conduct a Weekly Project Review to keep tasks and the Project Team on track • Create and protect time to do your own Project Work • Design and implement Project Meetings and various forms of communication	✔ Weekly Project Reviews ✔ Project Meeting Agendas
6. **Close & Codify the Project**	• Gather ongoing data to help inform outcomes • Facilitate a Project Debrief to consider successes and challenges • Codify learnings for the future	✔ Formal and Informal Project Feedback ✔ Project Debrief ✔ Project Codification Plan

3

PLAN THE PROJECT—
Excel, Google Sheets,
and More, Oh MY!

In this chapter, you will learn to:
- Determine which Project Planning tool is most effective for you
- Decide which Project Columns are necessary for your project
- Create Project Buckets to begin chronological project thinking
- Break down Project Buckets into Project Tasks

Now that you've created your Statement, drafted your Summary, gotten clear on Roles & Responsibilities--and maybe even created Job Descriptions, collected input, and built investment--it's time to get a lot more granular, and focus on the reason you likely picked up this book to begin with. Let's build that Project Plan, shall we?

We are finally here, down to the level of detail where many of us are accustomed to starting at! Insert drumroll! The Plan! Before we jump into the Project Plan (sslloooww down, my Google Sheet lovers!), there is a process to get us to the best outcome.

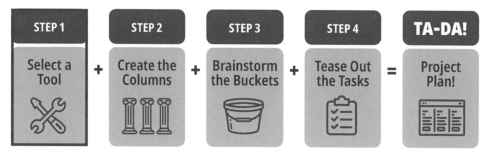

STEP 1		STEP 2		STEP 3		STEP 4		TA-DA!
Select a Tool	+	Create the Columns	+	Brainstorm the Buckets	+	Tease Out the Tasks	=	Project Plan!

Principles to Consider When Selecting a Project Management Tool

- **Simpler is better.** Don't be scared to use something very rudimentary if your project is simple enough and includes just a few people.

- **Familiarity is important.** This is not the time to roll out a brand-new app or snazzy piece of software. More important than any tool is how you USE the tool, and this part should be easy!

- **Accessibility is key.** Ideally, you are in and out of this Plan a lot, so make sure it's easy to access.

SELECT THE RIGHT PROJECT MANAGEMENT TOOL

This chapter may be why you picked up this book in the first place! How on earth do you choose a good Project Planning tool? There are a ton of different options out there, and every one will vie for your attention. Some are incredibly simple and intuitive, while others require formal training and certification. If your project is reasonably complex, you will want your tool to sort and filter by date and by owner (at least!), so you can easily monitor progress and assign tasks. If your project is simpler, you may be able to get away with a simple table and several columns of information.

If you need a few more questions to prompt your thinking, here is a list to help:

How simple or complex is my project?

Is there some information I will need to sort and filter?

How will I want to access my Project Plan?
Just from my computer or do I need it on my phone as well? Does the whole organization need access via a web-based tool?

Am I the sole author of my Project Plan or will others write and update, too?

Who else needs to regularly review my Project Plan?

What organizational tools we are already committed to?

How will I personally view my Project Plan?
Mobile or hard copy?

Do I want to sort and filter my project dates and tasks?

Your answers to these questions will start to guide you in the direction of which tool to pick for a particular project. Keep in mind that not all projects require the same level of tool. Ultimately, you will want several tools in your project toolkit so you can select the most appropriate option for each project.

Kelly's project is relatively complex and complicated. Her district already firmly lives in the Google-verse, so Kelly selects Google Sheets for her Plan. This way, it's compatible with other district tools, familiar to her team and Stakeholders, and easy to access and share.

Possible Project Management Options:

- ❏ A simple table in MS Word or a Google Doc
- ❏ MS Excel or Google Sheets
- ❏ Fancier project management software like Asana, Trello, or Basecamp

What Project Management tool will you use for your project? Why did you make this choice?

Now that your Project Management tool is selected, let's begin to customize it for your particular project. We will start with choosing the columns—or basic information—we want about each step of our project.

Project Plan: Articulates the goals, tasks, owners, and resources to accomplish the outcomes of a particular project. It clearly defines all work related to the project and who is in charge of various project pieces.

SELECT YOUR PROJECT COLUMNS

If I asked you to rattle off information you wanted to know about your project at any given time, you would probably quickly say, "Task, Deadline, Owner." Indeed, yes! But you may want a little bit more information about each of those Project Tasks, such as Start Date or Status or Other Resources. I call this, "Selecting the Right Project Columns."

Kelly's Tutoring Program

Kelly carefully selected which "columns," or sets of information, she wanted to see in her project plan. She chose more over less given the complexity of her project.

Bucket	Task	Owner	Helpers	Status
General	Project team launch	Kelly		Complete
General	Finalize project plan	Kelly	Project team	Complete
General	Write & send weekly project team email	Kelly		Complete
Principal Engagement	Preview project during Principal Manager huddle	Kelly	Frank	Complete
Budget	Confirm budget	Kelly	Tonya	Complete
General	Write & send weekly project team email	Kelly		Complete
Principal Engagement	Write & submit project launch message for weekly principal blast	Kelly	Frank	Complete

3.1 Kelly's Tutoring Project Columns

Kelly's choice of Project Columns allows her to sort information by deadline (so she can see upcoming due dates), by owner (so she can send out Project Assignments), by Status (so she can celebrate progress or look for delays), and by Project Bucket (more on that one in the next section.)

Your view will depend on what information you want about the project. At a minimum, your Project Columns will include:

- Task
- Owner
- Helpers
- Deadline
- Status
- Notes / Questions

You may add additional columns, such as:

- Notes
- Resources
- Start Date

**What Columns will your Plan include?
List them here.**

Now that we know what information we will track across our plan, let's consider our workstreams. which we will call Project Buckets—the big categories of our work.

> **Project Bucket:** The larger categories of a project that contain smaller tasks within. For example, Kelly will assign tasks related to the Project Buckets of budget, facilities, and training.

CONSIDER THE PROJECT BUCKETS

STEP 1		STEP 2		STEP 3		STEP 4		TA-DA!
Select a Tool	+	Create the Columns	+	Brainstorm the Buckets	+	Tease Out the Tasks	=	Project Plan!

While it may LOOK easy to just start brainstorming a million steps into a Google Sheet, Excel table, or special app, our brains actually revolt a bit when we try to do this. They want us to think about the bigger stuff first, so we can organize the smaller stuff accordingly.

Kelly's Tutoring Program

It's easier for Kelly to list out all the Project Tasks related to each of her buckets by category — including Budget, Curriculum, Tutoring Hiring, and Tutor Training — before she makes the steps chronological and assigns them to others.

Project Bucket	Budget	Curriculum	Tutor Hiring	Tutor Training
Project Tasks	• Confirm budget • Build a budget projection (known costs, variable costs) • Prepare monthly budget to actual reports	• Identify criteria for selecting curriculum • Research curriculum options • Schedule demos for top 3-4 curriculum options • Share curriculum options with 3-4 principals; get feedback • Recommend a curriculum decision; secure approval from CAO • Purchase selected curriculum	• Read past drafts of tutor job descriptions • Draft tutor job description • Circulate tutor job description for feedback • Post Tutor role to internal hiring boards (e.g., district teacher newsletter) • Post Tutor role with external hiring boards • Secure two other interviewers • Identify interviewers' availability for interviews • Design a scheduling process	• Draft tutor training scope and sequence; get feedback • Finalize tutor training scope and sequence • Schedule tutor trainings • Draft 25% of tutor training lesson plans • Draft 50% of tutor training lesson plans • Reserve space for tutor trainings • Draft 75% of tutor training lesson plans • Draft 100% of tutor training lesson plans • Order meals/snacks for tutor trainings • Finalize tutor training lesson plans • Print handouts for tutor trainings • Lead tutor trainings

3.2 Kelly's Project Tasks

List your buckets in the following spaces. Visual learners, you may want to grab your Post-Its!

Common Project Buckets

Budget/Finance	Logistics	Decisions to Be Made
Facilities	Purchasing	
Technology	Vendors	Onsite/ Day of Execution
Communications	Research	

With these Project Buckets in place, it's easier to break down the Tasks within each category. We'll do one together in the next section of this book.

Now that you know your Project Buckets, it's time to break things down into actual, bite-sized Project Tasks. Yup, this is it! The moment you've been waiting for!

Potential Project Pitfall:

Once you get the obvious buckets listed, you might notice some "secret buckets" emerge. Ooooooh, secret buckets, you ask? Whatever could they be? Well, they are not a secret from you, dear reader. Triple check your Plan for the following buckets:

- **Decisions To Be Made.** Given all the actions that swirl around decisions, it is good to call these out. Consider any key decisions for your project. There may even be micro-decisions within these larger decisions.

- **Feedback Cycles.** If your project is new, controversial, or complicated, you'll want to build in time to request input from others and then incorporate time in to iterate, research, and so on. For example, you may want to include dates you are collecting feedback and time to incorporate the input.

- **Communications.** Depending on your project's level of complexity, you may want to call out Communications as its own bucket. For example, if you'll need to report to the board on a decision, let's get that out there now.

BREAK THE PROJECT BUCKETS INTO TASKS

This section will guide you through breaking down Buckets into Tasks, by getting your To-Dos into the most specific size possible.

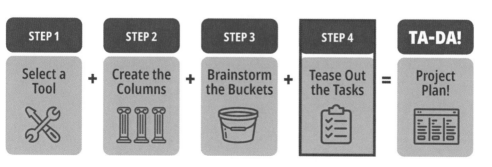

> **Project Tasks:** The steps that make your project run smoothly. Ideally, each task is discrete, assigned to an owner, and adds up to the larger whole of the project. Project Tasks are what you will check on a daily basis to keep your project moving.

Let's jump back to Kelly's project.

Kelly's Tutoring Program

One of Kelly's Project Buckets is Tutor Hiring. To brainstorm her bite-sized Project Tasks, Kelly needs to ask herself:

- When do I need to have the tutors hired by?
  (Consult with members of the HR team.)
- What materials need to be created?
  (Check for what we already have.)
- How will they be hired?
  (Should we interview in person or via Zoom?)
- What data needs to be collected?
  (Does the HR team need anything?)
- How do we advertise for the role?
  (What procedures need to be followed?)

Kelly then creates the list of Tasks that fall in her Hiring Bucket:

- Read past drafts of tutor job descriptions
- Draft new tutor job description
- Circulate for input from manager and HR team
- Post tutor role in district teacher newsletter
  (Flag! Find out when this goes out!)

- Post tutor role with external hiring sources
  (What are these? Do we have district accounts? Can I post?)
- Secure two more interviewers
- Identify interviewer availability
- Figure out scheduling process and identify any software used
- Write interview script *(Who will want input here?)*
- Create templates for communication with candidates
  (Does anyone need to approve?)

How teeny-tiny should my Project Tasks be?

Honestly, make them as small as possible. Here's why:

1. You want to be able to pluck them off your Project Plan, block time on your calendar tackle them, and then knock them out. This will be easier if they are short and sweet.

2. If you are assigning Tasks to other people, keeping them small will help you be as clear as possible.

Break down one of your Project Buckets into a set of Project Tasks. Pick your hardest bucket first. Continue this process for all of your Buckets until you have a document with a LOT of steps or a wall covered in Post-Its. Once we know ALL of our Tasks across ALL of our Buckets, it's time to sequence them!

MAKE THOSE PROJECT TASKS CHRONOLOGICAL

With your big stack of Tasks on hand, you have some options on how to land them into a coherent Project Plan. This is what you will use to actually guide your work on a daily basis.

Option 1: Go into the Project Management tool you selected earlier in the chapter, and just start adding all of your Tasks.

Option 2: If you are a visual planner, you could lay your Tasks out onto a calendar first. Seeing the steps laid out on an actual calendar will allow you to coordinate with other key organizational deadlines, holidays, and activities. No one wants a million project due dates right after a three-day weekend, right?

Kelly's Tutoring Program

Let's look at Kelly's full Project Plan together. (You can also see a full digital version over at thetogetherpress.com/the-together-project-manager.) Note how Kelly broke down her Project Tasks at a high level of detail.

Bucket	Task	Owner	Helpers	Status
General	Project team launch	Kelly		Complete
General	Finalize project plan	Kelly	Project team	Complete
General	Write & send weekly project team email	Kelly		Complete
Principal Engagement	Preview project during Principal Manager huddle	Kelly	Frank	Complete
Budget	Confirm budget	Kelly	Tonya	Complete
General	Write & send weekly project team email	Kelly		Complete
Principal Engagement	Write & submit project launch message for weekly principal blast	Kelly	Frank	Complete

3.3 Kelly's Tutoring Project Columns

As you can see, Kelly's Project Tasks have a few common criteria:

- Each Project Task **starts with an action-oriented verb**, like "Schedule," "Create," or "Order."
- Every single Task **has a clear Owner**. Nothing is dual-ownership or blank.
- Each Task **has a clear deadline** and a note, if needed, about larger organizational or calendar issues.

Real Deadlines vs. Flexible Deadlines?

You may be wondering what a REAL deadline is versus the more flexible deadlines. Great question!

In Kelly's case with the Saturday Tutoring Program, a REAL deadline is securing space for their training. This is a real deadline because there is a process in place to reserve large district training spaces, and if Kelly wants to host the training in November—before the program begins in January—she needs to abide by the September 1 deadline for space requests. A *(slightly more)* flexible deadline is one such as developing the tutor training agenda, and of course, this needs to be completed in time to share it with the tutors. However, when she selects this deadline, she has more choice in the matter!

FAQ

What if I have to add Project Tasks to my Project Plan ongoing?

You will definitely have to add in Project Tasks, and we would encourage you to be as flexible as you can. The beauty of a detailed Project Plan is it will increase your flexibility and reliability as a Project Manager. For example, when a set of new Project Tasks emerges, you will be able move items around and communicate accordingly.

Now pull up a good chair and dump all of those Project Tasks into your tool of choice. Remember--you will need to sort Project Tasks in various ways, move steps around as things change (which they will, we PROMISE!), and communicate easily with others, so double-check your choice of Project Tool to make sure it works for you and your team!

Just remember, the more people you include in your Project Plan, both up-front and ongoing, the more complex it will be to manage. That is totally okay, and can be important for investment, but be sure to get your head around how you will actually USE your plan on a regular basis. You might try sharing screens or projecting the plan onto a wall to do real-time editing together during meetings.

Check, check, check! Okay, your Project Plan is in place and ready to move. Take a moment to read through your entire plan and make sure:

- **You can sort easily by Project Bucket.** This is helpful when you need to see groupings related to a specific area.
- **You can sort easily by person.** This will be helpful when you send out assignments to others.
- **You can sort easily by day and week.** This will be helpful for forecasting upcoming work.
- **You know how and when you will share your plan with others.**

Any edits? Okay, cool. Now that we have a Plan thoroughly in place, it is time to launch that project right out into the world. In this next section, we will focus on the big kick-off!

	CHAPTER OBJECTIVES	TOGETHER TOOL
1. **Prime the Project**	• Ask yourself useful Project Pre-Work Questions • Draft a Project Statement to align with your Participants • Write a Project Summary to finalize the project	✔ Project Statement ✔ Project Summary
2. **Create Clear Project Roles & Responsibilities**	• Get clear about the actual project work that needs to be done • Figure out who is best positioned to take on which tasks • Determine how to communicate about the project work with your Participants	✔ Clear Roles and Responsibilities ✔ Project Job Description
3. **Plan the Project**	• Determine which Project Planning tool is most effective for you • Decide which Project Columns are necessary for your project • Create Project Buckets to begin chronological project thinking • Break down Project Buckets into Project Tasks	✔ Project Plan
4. **Launch the Project**	• Differentiate your project communication for various Project Stakeholders • Determine your method for launching your project into the world	✔ Project Communications Chart ✔ Project Launch Agenda ✔ Project Launch Emails
5. **Manage Yourself & Others**	• Conduct a Weekly Project Review to keep tasks and the Project Team on track • Create and protect time to do your own Project Work • Design and implement Project Meetings and various forms of communication	✔ Weekly Project Reviews ✔ Project Meeting Agendas
6. **Close & Codify the Project**	• Gather ongoing data to help inform outcomes • Facilitate a Project Debrief to consider successes and challenges • Codify learnings for the future	✔ Formal and Informal Project Feedback ✔ Project Debrief ✔ Project Codification Plan

4

LAUNCH THE PROJECT— Or Let's Get the Project Party Started!

In this chapter, you will learn to:
- Differentiate your project communication for various Project Stakeholders
- Determine your method for launching your project into the world

With our people primed up and our plans built in detail, let's launch this project with pizazz! Too often we jump right into execution without carefully considering who we want to get excited, how we'll keep them motivated, and when we'll communicate with them along the way. No longer!

Our first step: Creating a Communications Chart! The Communications Chart will be used to carefully map out who is impacted and how to most effectively communicate with them at the beginning and throughout the project. After completing the Communications Chart (either solo or with your Project Participants), you will fold these new communication tasks right into. . . you guessed it! The Project Plan!

> **Project Communications Chart:** A table that identifies your Project Team and Project Stakeholders considers how to approach them, and plans for ongoing communications.

As always, select only which pieces of Project Planning make the most sense for your project. Not every project needs every step!

And why on earth take the time to create this Communications Chart? If we don't systematically consider all of the individuals and groups impacted by our project from every angle, someone is inevitably forgotten or not given the right information, thus derailing the entire project. We recommend running your Communications Chart by other members of your Project team or even completing it together!

CREATE A PROJECT COMMUNICATIONS CHART

Before we just jump into emailing people with To-Dos and success stories all willy-nilly and wild-like (#guilty), we want to plan your overall strategy for communicating with your project team, partners, and involved others. This means thinking through every part of your project from each different person's shoes. This is important because projects impact people in different ways: whether requiring their time, their resources, their expertise—or heck, even their emotional involvement.

Kelly will help us by modeling how to complete the entire Communications Chart section by section. But we'll also provide you, our dear reader, opportunities to stop and conduct your OWN brainstorming. Of course, if it's more helpful, you could read through our entire example FIRST, and then complete your own chart in one big swoop! Your call, but either way, let's get ready to communicate!

IDENTIFY YOUR PROJECT STAKEHOLDERS

Let's start by naming WHO will be involved. In this case, we don't mean the Project Participants; we're thinking through anyone who is impacted by the actual project. Maybe they host a tutoring site? Maybe they play a role in curriculum selection? Maybe they need to ensure the tutors get paid?

Kelly needs to consider:

- School building principals?
- Facilities people?
- Families and parents?
- District teams, such as HR?

Kelly drops them all into the Communications Chart that follows.

Stakeholders (Individuals & Groups)	Initial Project Approach	What I need them to know, feel, or do?	How? (Email, Call, Meeting, Other)	When (or Frequency, if ongoing)
Principals				
Facilities				
Families/ Parents				
4.1 Project Communications Chart				

WHO is impacted by your project?
Think through every possible group and jot a list in the space provided.

ARTICULATE YOUR INITIAL PROJECT LAUNCH

Let's dig deeper into Kelly's vision for her FIRST interaction with each of these groups. We really want to put ourselves in their shoes and understand where and how a project could impact various people.

Let's take a look at Kelly's principals. For the most part, many of them will be excited about the extra academic support that the tutoring program provides. This is why Kelly plans for them to first hear about the tutoring program via the weekly principal memo from the district. However, there are a few principals she knows may be nervous about having multiple Saturday programs in their building at one time. For them, individual phone calls or email may be more helpful—before they read the news in the blast!

Who?	Principals
Initial Project Approach	<u>BY 8/14:</u> individual touchpoints with Principals Boone, Booker, and Hervey <u>8/14:</u> send preview in principal blast <u>8/21:</u> share overview during principal huddle
What I need them to know, feel, or do?	
How (e-mail, meeting, other)?	
When (date or frequency)?	
Other	

4.2A Kelly's Communications Chart

PUT YOURSELF IN YOUR STAKEHOLDERS' SHOES

This is where we really want to step back—even if for a quick five minutes—and imagine our project in the eyes of our Stakeholders. A few questions to help you with this were laid out previously.

Kelly's Tutoring Program

Kelly wants her district's principals to feel invested and excited about the new tutoring program and the ways it can help improve student results. She also wants them to take action by identifying possible tutors and helping enroll students from their own schools. In the principal blast, we can give examples of our desired tutoring results.

We can also create very easy ways for them to help recruit possible tutors and students to enroll. For example, we can create flyers for them to send home to parents directly and give them social media snippets for their school to put out.

Okay, now Kelly can pop this in her Communications Chart.

Who?	Principals
Initial Project Approach	BY 8/14: individual touchpoints with Principals Boone, Booker, and Hervey 8/14: send preview in principal blast 8/21: share overview during principal huddle
What I need them to know, feel, or do?	KNOW: Updates & upcomings DO: Lead student recruitment & registration
How (e-mail, meeting, other)?	
When (date or frequency)?	
Other	

4.2B Kelly's Communications Chart

> **What do you want each party to know? How do you want them to feel? What do you need them to do? What's your plan to address them?**

Our last step is to take some serious specific actions. We need to define how and when these communications will happen, so we can add relevant deadlines and meetings right into our Plan! Boom!

DETERMINE THE HOW/WHEN OF YOUR PROJECT COMMUNICATION

Kelly's Tutoring Program

- It is unlikely Kelly can write one weekly Project Team update that meets everyone's needs, so she needs to tap into existing communication channels and also think more about cadence.
- Kelly can imagine the facilities team doesn't need to hear from her each week. And goodness knows people do not need another email in their lives.
- Kelly is pretty sure the central operations team sends a weekly blast to facilities people, and she knows the superintendent sends a bi-weekly update to principals.

This is now enough information for Kelly to think of the how she wants to communicate with them ongoing.

Who?	Principals
Initial Project Approach	<u>BY 8/14:</u> individual touchpoints with Principals Boone, Booker, and Hervey <u>8/14:</u> send preview in principal blast <u>8/21:</u> share overview during principal huddle
What I need them to know, feel, or do?	<u>KNOW:</u> Updates & upcomings <u>DO:</u> Lead student recruitment & registration
How (e-mail, meeting, other)?	Brief blurbs in Principal email blast Training to review recruitment & registration process & tools October 30 Principal meeting
When (date or frequency)?	
Other	

4.2B Kelly's Communications Chart

Jot your HOW and WHEN into your Communications Chart. Now rinse and repeat for each of your Stakeholders.

And if it helps, here is Kelly's completed Communications Chart:

Who?	Initial Project Approach	What I need them to know, feel, or do?	How (e-mail, meeting, other)?	When (date or frequency)?
Project Team	• By 7/28: launch meeting via video call	**Do:** Assigned action items	Email summary	After weekly project team meetings
		Feel: Invested in the project	Shout outs Handwrite thank you notes to individual teammates	During weekly project team meetings After they complete major milestones
Principals	• By 8/14: individual touchpoints with Principals Boone, Booker, and Hervey • 8/14: send preview in principal blast • 8/21: share overview during principal huddle	**Know:** Updates & upcomings	Brief blurbs in Principal email blast	Weekly
		Do: Lead student recruitment & registration	Training to review recruitment & registration process & tools	October 30 Principal meeting
Facilities	• Partner with Helen to share overview during next facilities team meeting	**Do:** Support facilities needs	Ask for review and feedback on facilities needs plan	During bi-weekly facilities team meetings
		Feel: Invested in the project	Share registration numbers & impact	During bi-weekly
Families	• November: Virtual information sessions hosted by campus leaders	**Know:** Benefits of the program	Virtual information sessions	November 10 – 15
		Do: Register their students	Reminders through school newsletter	Weekly

4.3 Kelly's Communications Chart

What if I am new in my role and have no idea who is impacted by my project?

Ask, ask, and ask some more. Make it part of every meeting to ask. . . Who will have feelings about this project? Why/How are they impacted? Who often gets forgotten in communication? Who just likes to know what is happening?

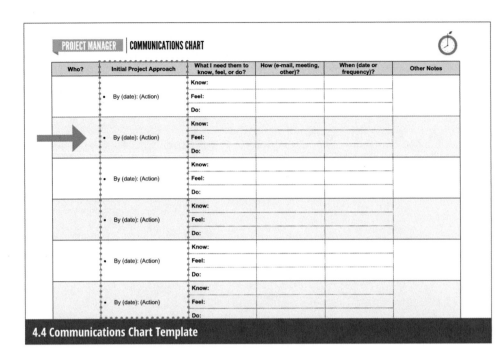

Who?	Initial Project Approach	What I need them to know, feel, or do?	How (e-mail, meeting, other)?	When (date or frequency)?	Other Notes
	• By (date): (Action)	Know: Feel: Do:			
	• By (date): (Action)	Know: Feel: Do:			
	• By (date): (Action)	Know: Feel: Do:			
	• By (date): (Action)	Know: Feel: Do:			
	• By (date): (Action)	Know: Feel: Do:			
	• By (date): (Action)	Know: Feel: Do:			

PROJECT MANAGER | COMMUNICATIONS CHART

4.4 Communications Chart Template

PROJECT COMMUNICATIONS CHART

I know, I know, a Project Communications Chart can feel so. . . extraneous. Can't we just DO the work now? Sure, but skipping this step can have a huge impact on your project's results. Remember, they are called PROJECTS for a reason. Because they are collaborative, complex, and take a group to complete them. One blindsided Project Stakeholder can grind the entire project to a halt. I don't want to scare you, but let's say you realize way too late that the facilities team is completely tapped out with other school events on tutoring days. . . Gulp. We don't want that, so let's ensure we are thoughtfully bringing people along with us.

Now that you've drafted your Project Communications Chart, you need to make sure you have time to actually work it. If you are writing a weekly update to a particular group, block time on your calendar to do so. We will dive deeper into managing yourself and others on Project Steps in Chapter 5. Let's launch this project, shall we?

PREPARE A PROJECT LAUNCH

Now it's time to thoughtfully launch this whole thing. Let's return to that initial touchpoint column of your Communications Chart.

You will likely have two types of ongoing Project Communications—to your Project Team (the people actually working on the project with you) and to your Project Stakeholders (those who are impacted.) Let's take them one by one.

Obviously, your Launch should match the overall size and scope of your project, but there are a few reasons to create some splash. A great Launch can:

- Get everyone on the same page at the same time
- Build energy around the outcome or mission of the project
- Harness excitement to complete a large amount of the project early on

There are many ways you can launch your project, including but not limited to:

- A pre-project survey that polls people about their opinions of the project
- An overview email, including a rallying cry or motto
- A video call to help surface why people are excited and what questions they have
- An in-person meeting to do all of the above, but also possibly build in a working session to refine the project plan together or complete other group tasks

As you determine your approach, consider:

- How well does your Project Team know each other?
- How familiar are they with the project and ways to achieve the outcomes?
- How familiar are they with their own roles?
  Is there any pre-work that could help get them up to speed?
- How excited and motivated are they by the topic?

KELLY'S PROJECT TEAM LAUNCH

If you answered the previous questions and realized your Project Team had a lot of enthusiasm and background knowledge, the lower-key your Launch can be. But be careful not to take people's excitement for granted. In most organizations, no one has "extra time" to support other projects. People are figuring how to squeeze this project in, either because they are excited by the topic OR they have been "voluntold" to do it. (What is "voluntold," you may ask? Well, think about it. Exactly!).

If you frequently lead projects across your organization, keeping people excited to work on project teams with you is very helpful. In my own previous jobs, where I had exactly no extra capacity, there was one particular project manager to whom I couldn't resist saying yes. She made my role in the project easy, fun, and constantly connected our work to the mission. Heck, she even made a motto and team t-shirts!

Kelly launches her tutoring program with a video call to ensure:

- All Participants can meet each other
- Enough time for an overview of key timelines and deliverables
- Excitement about the mission and impact of the Tutoring Program
- Space to share her vision for the Project Team's collaboration

To pull this off, Kelly needs to:

- Find a date and time that works for everyone
- Share her reasoning for a video call (too much travel for people to all leave their offices and come in person)
- Create an agenda that supports her desired outcome
- Pre-meet with anyone who may have questions or concerns about the project

Let's preview her actual agenda next.

CRAFT YOUR LAUNCH AGENDA

No matter how you approach your project kick-off, you will want to prepare some kind of agenda to guide you. This is important because you are trying to create a feeling of excitement and a strong sense of action. None of this happens by accident, and we want to carefully plan it in advance, so we can be more flexible and react in the moment.

Time	Agenda	Facilitation Notes
Pre-Work		• Read the Project Statement and Project Summary, and bring any clarifying or probing questions
10 min	Welcome to our project team 😊	• Open: why I'm excited about this project • Round robin: introduce yourself, your role on the team, and one thing that makes you excited about this project
10 min	Get invested in the big picture: Project Statement & Project Summary	• Clarifying questions (who, what, when, and where questions) • Probing questions (how and why questions)
10 min	Defining Success	• What does success look like for this project? • How might we measure it? ○ *Note: this is a brainstorm conversation; will dig into further detail during our next team meeting.*

20 min	Project Plan Review	• *5 min silent review of the plan*
		• 5 min: Clarifying or probing questions
		• Discuss and revise the plan as needed:
		  ○ What tasks are we missing?
		  ○ Do we need to adjust the "owners" of any tasks?
		  ○ What tasks are scheduled out of order?
		  ○ Are there any dependencies between tasks that we need to be aware of?

10 min	Project Team Communications	• How will we update on progress? How will we report what is on and off track?
		  ○ Propose: everyone updates the project plan 24 hrs prior to team meetings; if we need to communicate between projects, tag using @ comments in the project plan
		  ○ Communication preferences: what's the best way to communicate with you 1:1 (phone, email, text)

10 min	Scheduling	• Schedule dates/times and send invites for standing team meeting • Determine whether any team members need 1:1 meetings
5 min	Closing	• What's one thing you are looking forward to?

4.5 Kelly's Project Team Launch Agenda

Kelly includes a few key components in her initial meeting:

- Team building and connection to the project mission
- Space for collaboration
- Time for questions
- Alignment on future interactions

But what about people who just need to know what is happening—even if they don't play an active role in working on the project? Read on!

> **What is your Project Launch plan for your Project Team and why?** Sketch out your agenda or pre-meeting topics on your own or check out our starter Together Templates at <u>thetogetherpress.com/the-together-project-manager</u>.

> **What if you have a reluctant Project Team Member?**
>
> You will! This is a natural part of group dynamics and the project management process. Take time to get to know this team member, their hopes and fears, and strategize together about how you can invest them in the purpose and the project. Differentiating project assignments will help you flex your project management skills!

STAKEHOLDER PROJECT LAUNCH

Now that you know when and how you are communicating to the Project Team, you will likely end up doing some aspect of the communications in writing. Let's ensure that our writing is clearly tailored to the overall audience. Only you know the culture of your organization, but let's consider how we can make your communication:

- Simple
- Readable
- Predictable
- Progress-orientated
- When appropriate, celebratory

As you may recall, Kelly decided to send her Project Communication to the principals through an existing email blast. This requires her to submit an update in writing through the Superintendent's Chief of Staff in advance, so the format is somewhat dictated for her.

Kelly's Tutoring Program

Here's how Kelly set up her update to principals to ensure it was simple and readable.

Subject: **Saturday Tutoring Program Project Preview**   Priority ⌄

Calibri (Body) ⌄ 11 ⌄ A ⌄   B *I* U̲ ab 🖊 ⌄ x² x₂   ☰ ☷ ☰ ⌄ ⇥ ⇤   ∘∘∘

Hello Principals!

I hope this message finds you well and gearing up for the school year ahead—we are excited to welcome scholars back into your buildings later this month! Today, I'm writing to preview a new project we will be planning for this fall and launching next spring: a Saturday Tutoring Program.

Context:

- We are launching a district-wide Saturday Tutoring Program because we believe that extra academic support is a key component of students' academic success. Our big goal is that 100% of participating students will meet their individual academic growth goals.
- You can review a high-level planning timeline in our project statement

What you can expect:

- Your primary role in this project will be leading student recruitment & registration for the program.
  Our project team will support you through this process throughout the fall.
- We will be attending the August 21 Principal Huddle to provide a more detailed overview of the program and next steps. If you have questions you'd like us to answer during this time, please submit them through this form.

If you have any pressing questions in the meantime, please don't hesitate to reach out.
On behalf of our project team, we look forward to working with you!

Best,

- Kelly, Assistant Director of Student Support—Project Lead
- Frank, Managing Director of Student Support—Project Sponsor
- Helen, Facilities Director
- Pablo, Assistant Director of Teaching and Learning
- Tonya, Manager of Student Support Finances
- Dante, Assistant Director of Data and Analytics

4.6 Kelly's Weekly Email Update to Principal Stakeholders

What is your Project Launch plan for your Project Stakeholders and why? Sketch out your agenda or pre-meeting topics on your own or check out our starter Together Templates at <u>thetogetherpress.com/the-together-project-manager</u>.

You can see that Kelly carefully included bullets, hyperlinks, and links to other relevant project documents, such as the Project Statement.

Including this in your communications can be a useful way to anchor updates in the bigger picture, show progress, and continue to build investment.

Pull out your calendar (and for more on that, take a look at *The Together Leader* or *The Together Teacher!*) and block time for any Project Communications work. For example, if you write a Weekly Project Update to principals that needs to go out on Fridays, but also requires pre-approval, you may need to block an hour on your calendar every Tuesday to write the update and time on Wednesdays with your manager to review, so that it's ready for submission to the superintendent's chief of staff each Thursday. You'll also want to consider how and when you'll keep in touch with your internal Project Team. Block time for this on both your calendar and your Project Plan.

You've been super thoughtful about Project Launch, and you're feeling confident and ready to go. Right!? Our next chapter is about helping you manage YOURSELF toward project outcomes—and supporting others along the way.

TUESDAY	WEDNESDAY	THURSDAY
11	12	13

Saturday Tutoring Program Weekly Priority: Strong Project Launch with Principals

Student Services Weekly Priority: Strong Start through Campus Onsites

Worktime: Student Support Services Fall Calendar	**Kelly and Jordan Check-in**	
Worktime: Write project launch message for weekly principal blast	Principal feedback: Saturday Tutoring Project Statement	**Submit project launch n**
Travel to campus	Travel to campus	Worktime: Beginning-of-Year Goal-setting
Yamin & Student Services Team: Campus Onsite	**Jazmin & Student Services Team: Campus Onsite**	Saturday Tutoring Program: Confirm Curriculum Selection Criteria
Kelly and LaTasha Check-in	**Frank & Kelly Check-in** Standing agenda item: Review project launch message for weekly	**Student Services Team Weekly Meeting**

4.7 Kelly's Project Communications in her Calendar

	CHAPTER OBJECTIVES	TOGETHER TOOL
1. **Prime the Project**	• Ask yourself useful Project Pre-Work Questions • Draft a Project Statement to align with your Participants • Write a Project Summary to finalize the project	✔ Project Statement ✔ Project Summary
2. **Create Clear Project Roles & Responsibilities**	• Get clear about the actual project work that needs to be done • Figure out who is best positioned to take on which tasks • Determine how to communicate about the project work with your Participants	✔ Clear Roles and Responsibilities ✔ Project Job Description
3. **Plan the Project**	• Determine which Project Planning tool is most effective for you • Decide which Project Columns are necessary for your project • Create Project Buckets to begin chronological project thinking • Break down Project Buckets into Project Tasks	✔ Project Plan
4. **Launch the Project**	• Differentiate your project communication for various Project Stakeholders • Determine your method for launching your project into the world	✔ Project Communications Chart ✔ Project Launch Agenda ✔ Project Launch Emails
5. **Manage Yourself & Others**	• Conduct a Weekly Project Review to keep tasks and the Project Team on track • Create and protect time to do your own Project Work • Design and implement Project Meetings and various forms of communication	✔ Weekly Project Reviews ✔ Project Meeting Agendas
6. **Close & Codify the Project**	• Gather ongoing data to help inform outcomes • Facilitate a Project Debrief to consider successes and challenges • Codify learnings for the future	✔ Formal and Informal Project Feedback ✔ Project Debrief ✔ Project Codification Plan

5

MANAGE YOURSELF & OTHERS— Let's Get the Work Done!

In this chapter, you will learn to:
- Conduct a Weekly Project Review to keep tasks and the Project Team on track
- Create and protect time to do your own Project Work
- Design and implement Project Meetings and various forms of communication

Okay, let's take a breath! Our Project is up and running, and we've successfully launched, secured our support team, and planned our communications. In this chapter, we'll focus on keeping our own heads on straight and supporting all of the people and teams involved along the way.

Let's jump into the most critical aspect of keeping your project running—a regular review of your project.

> **Project Review:** A dedicated time and specific process to review the status of all Project Tasks, preview and assign upcoming Project Tasks, prep for Project Meetings, and block time to accomplish your own Project Work.

WEEKLY (OR DAILY) PROJECT REVIEWS

The only way to truly keep your project moving is to conduct systematic Project Reviews on a daily or weekly basis. These will allow you to identify upcoming challenges and adjust your plans accordingly. And celebrate your successes! Most Together Project Managers use some sort of Weekly Project Review Checklist to:

- Mark off completed tasks and celebrate progress
- Identify upcoming Project Tasks and block time to complete them
- Identify upcoming Project Tasks for others and send out reminders, offers of support, or meeting invites to complete the work
- Predict schedule collisions or potentially delayed tasks so you can pivot and communicate accordingly

Now, you might be thinking (as I would be), "What the heck, Maia?!? You want me to block time off to PLAN the work (even more!) when I could actually be DOING the work???" Indeed, I do. You may be the only human with a full bird's eye view of your project. To keep pushing toward your desired outcome, you have to take about an hour each week to review your Plans backwards and forwards. Don't worry, we're going to show you how! Read on!

Convinced? Intrigued? Let's see how this works in action.

Kelly's Tutoring Program

In addition to the tutoring program, Kelly is managing other projects as well. She applies the same steps to all of her projects weekly. Here's her Project Review Checklist.

Connection! Meeting with Myself!

For those readers familiar with *The Together Leader* or *The Together Teacher,* your Project Review time can easily be added to your Meeting with Myself. One caveat—this may make your meeting a bit longer. It takes time to make time! And achieve strong results.

PROJECT MANAGER | **REVIEW CHECKLIST**

Project Name: Saturday Tutoring Program

Status Check

- **Review Project Plan from Last Week.** What was completed? What is missing?
- **Review Data Trackers.** Are we on track with registrations? Budget?

Look Ahead

- **Course-correct.** What tasks need to be added/adjusted to the Project Plan based on the current status?
- **Filter by Deadlines.** What tasks need to happen this week? Over the next month?
- **Filter by Buckets.** What dependencies exist between tasks happening this week? Over the next month?
- **Look for Off-Track Moments.** What could cause the project to get stuck?

Get it Together

- **Create Project Update and Task Assignments.** Send team weekly round-up email and prepare any project meeting agendas.
- **Communicate Clearly.** Send any updates or reminders to other stakeholders (e.g., registration data & next steps to principals)
- **Prep My Calendar/Weekly Worksheet.** Block worktimes and/or schedule meetings to complete my tasks.

5.1 Kelly's Project Review Checklist

As you can see, Kelly breaks her Project Review into three sections:

- **Status Check:** She starts by seeing where things are with Project Tasks and reviews any relevant data collections, such as student registration numbers. This is also a really good time to step back and ensure you are not simply COB (Checking Off Boxes) but thinking instead about how your project is meeting its purpose and goals.

- **Look Ahead:** After this review, Kelly is ready to filter by various criteria, such as deadlines and Project Buckets, so she can send out updates and anticipate what could go off track with her project. This matters because one Project Task can easily topple other Project Tasks, so you want to look at an entire Project Bucket at one time.

- **Get It Together:** This is when Kelly will communicate any Task Assignments for the week (more on that coming!), draft her project communications, and prepare any Project Meeting Agendas. She takes a good hard look at her own calendar, and blocks out time to get her tasks done!

Let's see this in action on her actual calendar in a weekly view, otherwise known as a Weekly Worksheet. A Weekly Worksheet is an hour-by-hour view of your Time and Tasks for the week ahead. If you are interested in learning more, definitely check out *The Together Leader*.

Worktime: Student Support Services Fall Calendar	Kelly and Jordan Check-in
Worktime: Write project launch message for weekly principal blast	Principal feedback: Saturday Tutoring Project Statement
Travel to campus	Travel to campus
Yamin & Student Services Team: Campus Onsite	Jazmin & Student Services Team: Campus Onsite

5.2 Kelly's Project Work Time in her Calendar

The Together Project Manager

When should I complete my Project Reviews? How long will they take?

Depending on how many Project Plans you need to review, you might block anywhere from 30 minutes to 3 hours. You will want to be in a quiet space surrounded with your Project Plans, your checklist, a calendar, and good WiFi access to send reminders as needed. This is also a good time to troubleshoot any issues that could go wrong in the near future. A lot of Project Managers do this review on Wednesdays or Thursdays, so they can firm up meetings and project steps for the following week.

Consider your own Project Management life.
Create your own Project Review Checklist and block time to conduct it each week. See the following for a starter Together Template, or find a downloadable version thetogetherpress.com/the-together-project-manager.

Depending on how many Project Plans you need to review, you might block anywhere from 30 minutes to 3 hours. You will want to be in a quiet space surrounded with your Project Plans, your checklist, a calendar, and good WiFi access to send reminders as needed. This is also a good time to troubleshoot any issues that could go wrong in the near future. A lot of Project Managers do this review on Wednesdays or Thursdays, so they can firm up meetings and project steps for the following week.

Now that you've blocked time for regular Plan review, we bet you also have your OWN project work to do. Let's head over to your calendar!

Project Name: _____

Status Check

- **Review Project Plan from Last Week.** What was completed? What is missing?
- **Review Data Trackers.** Are we on track? Budget?

Look Ahead

- **Course-correct.** What tasks need to be added/adjusted to the Project Plan based on the current status?
- **Filter by Deadlines.** What tasks need to happen this week? Over the next month?
- **Filter by Buckets.** What dependencies exist between tasks happening this week? Over the next month?
- **Filter by Owner.** Who do I need to provide additional support to and/or follow up with this week?
- **Look for Off-Track Moments.** What could cause the project to get stuck?

Get it Together

- **Create Project Update and Task Assignments.** Send team weekly round-up email.
- **Communicate Clearly.** Send any updates or reminders to other stakeholders (e.g., registration stats & next steps to principals).
- **Prep My Calendar/Weekly Worksheet.** Block worktimes and/or schedule meetings to complete my tasks.
- **Prep Project Meeting Agendas and Pre-Work (if applicable) for Next Week.** Share with attendees.

5.3 Project Review Checklist Template

CREATE AND PROTECT TIME ON YOUR CALENDAR FOR PROJECT WORK

Undoubtably, you have a lot more going on than JUST your own project. You have whole other parts of your job, additional projects, and if your role involves other humans, you're subject to the usual workplace emails, pop-by's, and other welcome and unwelcome interruptions. Much of our Project Work requires focus and concentration, so how can we protect our time (and mental energy!) to advance our project causes? Here are some strategies to help.

- **Communicate your Project Work to others**
  Whether you have regular check-ins with a manager, host team meetings with colleagues, or write any kind of updates to share your work with others, be sure to regularly bring up the project(s) you are working on, the time they are taking you, and the outcomes you are hoping for.

- **Ensure each Project Task is bite-sized and action-oriented.** Break your tasks down to be as small as you can. "Make interview rubric" is a lot harder to make progress on than "Revise questions 1—10 of initial phone screen interview." Make your Project To-Dos as tiny as you can to fit them in around the edges of your calendar.

- **Block Time on your Calendar for Project Work, both recurring and one-off tasks.** When you complete your Weekly Review (which you will want to block time for each week, how meta is THAT?!), you'll identify tasks that will take you time next week. For each one, ask yourself, "What materials will I need? What kind of workspace do I need to be in? Is this better completed collaboratively? What cognitive load level is this task?" And then place that task in the right spot on your digital calendar. Book all-day appointments to note any recurring events or deadlines. For example, if you write a weekly project update to a group of people, block out the time to do it. And while you're at it, use a template to make your life easier!

- **Resist the Urge of Distraction during Project Work Time.**
  Yes, yes, things happen, but many of our distractions are ones we can take some responsibility for changing. Deep in tough Project Work, and you find your inbox calling your name? I hear you. But if we give our projects the attention they deserve and make REAL progress, then we have to prime ourselves for the task at hand. Switch locations, turn off the Internet, and kiss your phone goodbye for an hour. Do whatever it takes to focus on the task at hand.

- **Rehearse what you will say when interrupted.**
  Of course you will be interrupted! We don't live and work in vacuums. But practice a standard line or two to say when the inevitable happens. Two of my favorites: "I would love to give you my complete and full attention, but it will take me 30 minutes to revise a document for a project deadline. Can I come by your desk at ___ o'clock?" and "I'm totally buried today, but if you email me, I can promise to get back to you tomorrow!"

Now that we've helped ourselves with our Project Reviews and protecting Project Work time, let's think more about helping others complete their work as well.

What happens when something goes waaaay off track?

Project Peril is inevitable. When we first learned to upload our eBooks on Amazon, we experienced an unexpected four-day delay. When things veer off track, here are a few ways to grab hold of the steering wheel:

- **Pre-identify areas where things can go off track**, such as decision-making, weather, or technology. Build in buffer time or create backup plans. If curriculum doesn't arrive in time, can you go pick it up somewhere else?
- **Practice calling Project Huddles to strategize**, recalibrate, and recommunicate with your team as needed.
- **Readjust your overall Project Plan** and move anything impacted by the delay or change.

HELP OTHERS COMPLETE THE WORK

As Together Project Managers, we often find ourselves needing to push the work ahead but relying on other Project Team members to own and support the work. But if we just chuck a task at another person and hope for the best, it's unlikely we'll get the outcome we want. We may need to prompt, push, pull, nudge, and do all kinds of heavy lifting for other people. Not because others are unwilling or unable; everyone is juggling A LOT, and we are the ones most intimately familiar with our project and all of its moving pieces. As the Project Manager, part of the job is to make it easy on our Participants to do the work. Yes, sometimes, that means more work for us. Trust me, though, it will lead to stronger results in the end. Instead of finding yourself stalled by other people holding up progress, you'll plan, delegate, and support your Project Team.

There are a few ways we can encourage others move the project along: leading project team meetings, giving project assignments, supporting decision making, and making clear recommendations.

CONSIDER HOSTING PROJECT MEETINGS— OR OTHER METHODS OF TOUCHING BASE

In addition to the Project Launch Meeting you hosted previously, you will likely need a regular touchpoint with your Project Team. This may take the form of an in-person meeting, a video conference, or it could simply be a weekly email to the team.

Here are some things to keep in mind as you consider your approach:

- **Determine the purpose of the touchpoint.**
  No one wants to meet just to meet. Is the purpose to inform? Inspire? Answer questions? Make decisions? All of the above. Get clear on the purpose of your touchpoints and then select options that support that goal.

- **Consider the complexity of the project.**
  Simple project? Fewer touchpoints. Complex or fast-moving project? Possibly more touchpoints.

- **Figure out who needs to be included when (and who doesn't.)** Not everyone needs to be invited to everything. Decide if some of your meetings can include fewer members of the team, or if some emails don't need to go to every participant.

Let's peer into Kelly's approach to see how she thinks of gathering her Project Team.

Kelly's Tutoring Program

Kelly decided, with her Project Team, that this project was new and complex enough that they would start with weekly video meetings to review status, inform others of upcoming tasks, and make decisions.

Your Project Team likely needs special gathering options too because no doubt there will be anticipating, trouble-shooting, and celebrating that your team will need to do together.

Kelly built a team of colleagues committed to the same goal, so as she thinks about these questions, she realizes:

- No, Kelly's Participants don't all know each other very well. Some also know the work of schools better than others.

- There is overlapping work related to tutor job descriptions, central and school site operations, and communications with principals. Because of this, Kelly plans for weekly meetings.

- Because team members are often working out of different locations, Kelly schedules video calls to prevent unnecessary travel across town.

- Ideally, Kelly doesn't want to facilitate the meetings entirely herself. Because their purpose is to share updates on progress, anticipate challenges, and plan communications, she builds in structures to take turns leading.

With this laid out, it makes sense for Kelly to think about a regular standing agenda for these meetings, and any needed pre- or post-work. Kelly's brainstorm sounds like this:

Pre-work? In advance of the meeting, I think I should ask people to send me updates on past steps and any adjustments to the Project Plan.

Logistics of the Meeting? I think we should have videos on, screen-share from my computer, and meet once a week.

During the meeting? I think we should open the Project Plan on my shared screen and do some . . .
- Celebrations of what we have accomplished?
- Previewing of the two weeks ahead?
- Identification of any roadblocks, bottlenecks, or delayed decisions?
- Drafting of upcoming communications?

After the Meeting? I want to keep people connected to what we are actually trying to accomplish, so I wonder if I can somehow send out something inspiring each week—a cool tutor resume, a student photo, or a short video of boxes of curriculum arriving. This would also honor the operational lift since there is so much behind the scenes work!

Based on this thinking, Kelly drafts a standing team meeting agenda to share with the Project Team.

Kelly will share this draft with her Project Team to see if it meets everyone's needs, and encourage them to provide feedback. Now let's think about your project and what it requires.

Time (45 min)	Agenda	Facilitation Notes	Discussion Notes
Pre-work – due 24 hrs. in advance		• Update our project plan to reflect progress; add comments that identify roadblocks, bottlenecks, and/or delayed decisions that we need to discuss and resolve as a group	
5 min	Welcome	• Round robin: Build and deepen personal working relationships by answering a different icebreaker question each week	
5 min	Celebrations & Gratitude	• Popcorn: What happened this week that we want to celebration and/or show gratitude to each other for?	

10 min	Project Plan Review & Updates	• Pre-work review: What roadblocks, bottlenecks, and/or delayed decisions do we need to discuss and resolve as a group?
		• Looking ahead:
		  ○ **Course-correct.** What tasks need to be added/adjusted to the Project Plan based on the current status?
		  ○ **Filter by Milestones.** What tasks need to happen this week? Over the next month?
		  ○ **Filter by Buckets.** What dependencies exist between tasks happening this week? Over the next month?
		  ○ **Look for Off-Track Moments.** What could cause the project to get stuck?	

20 min	Deep Dive	• *This will be a rotating topic each week; this time may be used to:*
		  ○ *Inform/Review: share information and gather feedback*
		  ○ *Discuss: collaboratively brainstorm*
		  ○ *Align: ensure coordination across multiple stakeholders*
		  ○ *Decide: agree on a path forward*
		  ○ *Collaborate: work real-time on a shared deliverable*	

5.4 Kelly's Standing Project Team Meeting Agenda

Reminder: Block time on your calendar to prepare for, host, and follow up on Project Meetings. It may help to get recurring invites on your calendar now!

Questions to Consider as You Plan Project Meetings:

- What is the purpose of your Project Meeting? Is it informational? Inspirational? Problem-solving?
- Based on the purpose, what is a reasonable cadence to hold your Project Meetings? (Hint: Pull up your Project Plan to see if any decisions or deliverables may require special meetings.)
- Does the Project Team know each other?
- If not, do you need to add time to build team?
- Do you have the right people in the room? (If not, this will lead to more meetings later!)
- Do you need to create space for "guest participants" to join occasionally?
- How interconnected are each team member's roles, buckets, and deadlines?
- Would the group ever benefit from co-working time?
- Where are each of the project participants based? Is it easy to gather in person?
- If not, do you need video or audio calls?
- How will you ensure equity of voice, participation, and contribution?
- Do you anticipate asking team members to complete any pre- or post-work?

PROJECT MANAGER	PROJECT TEAM WEEKLY MEETING AGENDA				

Time	Agenda	Facilitation Notes	Discussion Notes	Next Steps
Pre-work – due 24 hrs in advance				
	Welcome			
	Celebrations & Gratitude			
	Project Plan Review & Updates			
	Deep Dive			
	Closing & Next Steps			

5.5 Project Meeting Agenda Template

Draft a Project Meeting Agenda. Who do you need to ask for input? Where will you store this agenda? How will notes be taken and acted on? If it helps, we have included a modifiable version of our template online here thetogetherpress.com/the-together-project-manager, and you can take a quick peek at the next image.

A strong agenda works for a singular project meeting, but if your project is longer and somewhat predictable, you may need to draft a scope and sequence to defer some topics for later.

Project Meeting Scope and Sequence

You may realize you'll need to address items that come into place further into the future. Enter a Scope and Sequence!

This is simply shorthand for having a method of planning longer-term meeting topics. For Kelly, some important project ideas came up on tutor training; she doesn't want a discussion to blow up that week's meeting agenda, but she also doesn't want to dismiss them. Kelly managed this with a shared Google Doc Meeting Scope and Sequence. This gave Kelly and her teammates a place to record future discussion topics. Current meetings could stay focused on what mattered most, and everyone felt there was a time and place to flag issues they anticipated along the way.

Kelly predicts several upcoming discussion topics related to decision-making, budget, and school communication. Based on the district calendar and other project deadlines, she knows she can use the Deep Dive section of her Project Team meeting wisely.

Kelly then shares her Scope and Sequence document with her entire Project Team so they can see what is coming and when. She also invites them to add topics as needed. She uses her Scope and Sequence to drive her topics for her Project Meeting Agenda each week.

If applicable, create a **Project Scope and Sequence.** A template is available for you thetogether-press.com/the-together-project-manager.

Do you have any long-term meeting topics you can anticipate now?

PROJECT MANAGER	MEETING SCOPE AND SEQUENCE	
Month	Topics

5.6 Project Meeting Scope and Sequence Template

In addition to your Project Meetings, you will also likely send out written communications to your Project Team as well. Let's dive into how to structure those next.

SEND WEEKLY PROJECT ASSIGNMENTS

Throughout your project, you'll communicate with two different groups of people—those deeply involved (the Project Team), and those involved around the edges (Project Stakeholders). For the former (your Project Team), you probably put a system for this in place during your Project Launch. If not, go back and do this now! You may also be managing people helping with one-off tasks or helpers who need just a little more. . . help, shall we say?

Kelly's Tutoring Program

Kelly sends Weekly Project Assignments to both her immediate Project Team and to her occasional helpers. Let's look at examples of both kinds of communication, and how Kelly uses her Project Plan make these happen. Let's start with an email following a Project Meeting.

As you can see, Kelly sent a summary of the Project Team meeting that includes the following elements:

- **A dose of inspiration and celebration.** Don't underestimate this. People can get caught in the weeds, and they want to be part of something larger. Keep calling out the impact and purpose!

- **Hyperlinks to relevant resources.** Make the lives easier by connecting to relevant documents, like the Project Plan.

- **Assign clear next steps.** Kelly's ask to update the Project Plan is crystal clear, and as an added bonus, she includes a snippet of the project plan so no one has to click somewhere else to figure out what is next!

Kelly also needs to share individual assignments. Sometimes we can send these all out at the start of the project, but in other cases, there may be people pulled in for just a few certain tasks. Let's peek inside Kelly's email to Sam, a member of her Project Team.

Subject: **Tutoring Project Team Weekly Wrap-Up: Week of September 21** Priority ⌄

Calibri (Body) ⌄ 11 ⌄ A ⌄ B *I* U ab ✏ ⌄ x² x₂ ☰ ☰ ☰ ⌄ ☰ ☰ ∘∘∘

Hi, team!

Great conversation today in our team meeting today—it's so exciting to hear about the progress we've made. This program is truly starting to come to life!

A moment of inspiration

Today I had my first Principal 1:1 to build a prioritized student recruitment list—Dr. Johnson is so excited about the tutoring program and what it will mean for students!

Key action items for the next two weeks

As a reminder, please update our project plan to reflect your progress on these tasks at least 24 hours before our next team meeting.

Bucket	Tasks	Owner	Helpers	Status	Deadline	Notes & Questions to answer
Curriculum	Purchase selected curriculum	Pablo	Tonya	Almost complete	9/23	
Student Recruitment, Principal Engagement	Schedule Principal 1:1s to draft prioritized list of students to recruit	Kelly		In progress	9/30	
Budget	Prepare monthly budget to actual report	Kelly	Tonya	In progress	9/30	
Tutor Hiring	Read past drafts of tutor job descriptions	Kelly		Not started	10/2	
Evaluation	Design program evaluation: review potential student data sources, draft metrics	Dante	Kelly	In progress	10/2	@Dante, let me know if you want to set up a 1:1 to work on this
Tutor Hiring	Draft tutor job description	Kelly	Sam (HR)	Not started	10/5	

As always, please feel free to reach out if you've got any questions. Thanks again, team!

Kelly

5.7 Kelly's Weekly Email Update to Principal Stakeholders

Subject: **Tutoring Program Project: Update & Requested Actions**   Priority ⌄

Calibri (Body) ⌃ 11 ⌃ A ⌄ | B *I* U ab ✎ ⌄ x² x₂ | ☰ ☰ ☰ ⌄ ⇤ ⇥ | ○○○

Hi Sam,

I hope this finds you well! I'm excited that we've kicked off the process of hiring tutors for our new program. I'm writing to give you a quick status update and to preview asks for your support over the coming weeks, including a request for us to meet before 10/21. If it's helpful, you can also reference our project plan to see how our work together fits into the bigger picture!

FYI—updates on what I've done since last week:

- Read past drafts of tutor job descriptions

- Draft tutor job description

- Circulate tutor job description for feedback

Upcoming requests for you:

- By 10/8, could you please help me post the job description (will send by EOD tomorrow) to any hiring boards you would typically publish to?

- Before 10/21, I'd love to schedule a meeting with you to learn about best practices for scheduling candidates with interviewers to help inform how I design a scheduling process - my goal is to finalize the process by 10/23. When would be a good time for us to meet?

- By 10/23, could you share with me any communication templates you've used in the past? E.G., invitation to interview emails, interview confirmation emails, etc? I'm working to build my communication templates by 10/30.

Please don't hesitate to reach out with any questions. Thanks, and look forward to connecting soon!

Kelly

5.8 Individual Project Assignment Email

How will you share Project Assignments with your team? And don't forget to put this step into your Plan and block time on your calendar!

Kelly's email to Sam is clear and to the point. Here's what makes it so effective:

- **Connection to the bigger picture.** It can be really easy to just say, "Do this by X date." This leaves people at a disadvantage because they don't see the larger context. Re-link to the Project Statement or Summary—and the actual Project Plan, if relevant.

- **Share progress on open Project Tasks.** Kelly called this her FYI section, and she clearly described the work she had already done on the tutor job descriptions.

- **Name the upcoming requests.** Kelly has some requests for Sam, and she made them with clear deadlines. She also offered options for meetings, and asked for resources.

If I'm Sam, I feel crystal clear on what I'm being asked to do, and I also feel supported and connected.

You could also ask your Project Team how they prefer to receive assignments and updates. While you can't always differentiate for every member of the team, it is our role as Project Managers to ensure the work gets done through whatever means possible. One benefit of taking time each week or day to communicate like this is that it gives your team an opportunity to reflect and celebrate. Too often, we are working so quickly on various aspects of our project—not to mention the remainder of our actual jobs—that we forget to notice what's going well!

FAQ

What if a Project Participant is blowing deadlines?

Deadlines will get missed. People are busy with things other than our project (WHAT?!). When this happens, you want to address sooner rather than later, and from a place of curiosity rather than accusation. Name your concern neutrally and directly: "I noticed the job description wasn't completed today as planned. How can I help?" Be prepared to roll up your sleeves and dive into the work with your team member. Maybe they need you to provide samples or skeletons of the work product, some co-working time, or stronger interference from you to make time to do their work.

Other Methods to Help Move Project Tasks When Getting Stuck

- Gentle re-pings by forwarding original request

- Invest them in the why and impact of the outcome

- Offer to co-do the work during a meeting

- Tag into existing meetings that the Project Team Member has with someone else

- Schedule a meeting to conduct a "voiceover"

- Make it "multiple choice" to reduce heavy lifting

- Create a "plug & play" for them to fill in the blanks

- Ensure it is "one click" with no searching, meaning a crystal clear email that is easy to answer

With these supports in place, we'll take a special detour to a different kind of work—decision-making!

We've managed ourselves and we've supported others to take on the Project Tasks, but what about when there are choices to make? Decision-making is a key place projects can stall out. We need to have plans in place to push decisions forward! Here we go!

HELP OTHERS MAKE DECISIONS

In some cases, we may need to jump to push decisions and recommendations forward. In some cases, you will want to go a step beyond creating the time, space and environment for helping others complete the work. You may need to actually be the person asking the questions AND proposing the answers because other people can get busy, or stuck, or both. While this can be a significant amount of work, it will go a long way towards achieving your ideal outcome.

Kelly's Tutoring Program

Kelly is holding an upcoming decision about which curriculum to use. Alice, the CAO, was the final decision maker, but Kelly was the recommender. In this case, because Kelly knows how busy Alice is—and she is aware of the negative consequences if this choice gets stalled--Kelly wants to do everything in her power to make decision-making easy and painless for Alice.

Recommender	Decider
• "Packages" a single recommendation for the Decider • Sets the recommendation, decision, revision, and finalization timeline at the beginning of the project and communicates to all Stakeholders • Faithfully and accurately gathers input from all stated Input groups (but may make decisions regarding entire cohort or representative cohort)	• Schedules time to thoughtfully participate in the decision-making process • Plans and (to the extent possible) adheres to the pre-planned process • Provides clear rationale for any decisions that go against the recommendation and offers support to the Recommender when communicating with Stakeholders

5.8 Recommender vs. Decider Chart[3]

RECOMMENDER VS. DECIDER

The distinction between Recommender and Decider is incredibly helpful. Too often, this difference is not clear up front and Project Managers throw up their hands in frustration with decisions getting stuck.

Kelly is not the instructional expert herself, but if she just asks Alice to select a curriculum, Alice may not make time to do it. No dig on her; she is busy! Here are some ways Kelly, the Recommender, can help Alice, the Decider, get the job done:

- Email Alice with a table of questions to be answered so it's super simple for her to reply
- Interview others to understand past curriculum usage in the district and how decisions were made, and then make a recommendation to Alice

3. Used with permission from KIPP Texas Public Schools

- Schedule a meeting with Alice to talk through options together
- Help Alice see the timeline and rationale for decision-making by sharing the Project Statement

PUT YOURSELF IN THEIR SHOES

Kelly needs to put herself in Alice's shoes to help her finalize her decision by asking herself:

- What are the criteria she will use to make her decision? For example, is her interest budget? Efficacy? Training ease?
- Will she end up delegating this decision? If so, to whom does she typically turn?
- How does she like to make decisions? Does she prefer to dig into all of the details or get topline summaries only? Does she want research background?
- Does she need to check in with anyone else before she feels comfortable making a decision? If so, can we have that person in the room?
- How does she like information presented? For example, does she prefer tables? Charts? Verbal overviews?

Whatever Kelly discovers or discerns, she will want to do her homework because she needs this decision made ASAP.

Kelly takes a few hours and completes a Decision-Making Chart with the curriculum she researched—based on what the district already uses—and ranks the choices against the criteria. She brings this chart, with her ultimate recommendation, to her meeting with Alice.

Project Name: Saturday Tutoring Program

Decision: Which curriculum will our Saturday tutors use?

Decision-Making Criteria				
Criteria 1	**Criteria 2**	**Criteria 3**	**Criteria 4**	
Ease of Training	Cost	Past Track Record	Assessment	
Options	**Criteria 1**	**Criteria 2**	**Criteria 3**	**Criteria 4**	**Criteria 5**
Curriculum A	★★★	★★☆	★★★	★★☆	★★★
Curriculum B	★★☆	★☆☆	★★★	★★☆	★★☆
Curriculum C	N/A	★★☆	★★☆	★★★	★★☆
Recommendation	Curriculum A				
Rationale:	• Curriculum A has the overall strongest performance across our criteria. • Because Curriculum A is already in use at many of our schools, we have personal experience with their strong record of success. Additionally, our familiarity with it makes it significantly easier to support training. • While Curriculum A's cost is over our current budget, we have identified options for re-allocating enough funds from other line-items within our overall budget.				

5.9 Kelly's Tutoring Program Decision-Making Chart

Let's peek at Kelly's method for laying out the decision in a way that is supportive of Alice.

Doing this kind of pre-work will help move the decision ahead because Kelly has clearly:

- Carefully considered the available options
- Understood Alice's criteria for making a decision and assessed each piece of curriculum against the criteria (using a handy dandy graphic for ease of review)
- Listed the benefits and drawbacks of each choice

PROJECT MANAGER | **DECISION-MAKING CHART**

Project Name: _____

Decision: _____

Decision-Making Criteria				
Criteria 1	Criteria 2	Criteria 3	Criteria 4	Criteria 5

Options	Criteria 1	Criteria 2	Criteria 3	Criteria 4	Criteria 5	Benefits	Drawbacks	Supporting Materials
Option 1	★★★	☆☆☆						
Option 2								
Option 3								
Recommendation	Option ___							

Rationale:	• X • Y • Z

5.10 Project Decision Chart Template

Consider an upcoming project decision.
Complete our Decision-Making template
(or something of your own design) to package
the options for the Decider.

Back to your own project! Let's start by figuring out how to anticipate upcoming decision points. Pull up that Project Plan and ask yourself these questions to forecast what's ahead:

- What do people in my organization have a lot of opinions about?
- Are there any upcoming decisions without a clearly assigned Decider? What steps do I need to add to get clarity?
- What decisions are big enough that they could hold up the rest of my Project Process?

No doubt, Managing Yourself and Helping Others will take you time. LOTS of it. But the payoff of smooth project operations will make it all worth it for you in the long run. Part of being a Together Project Manager is doing whatever it takes to ensure all of the Project Tasks add up to the outcome you aimed for at the start. The Project Team can get stuck, lose sight of the larger goal, or end up with bottlenecks. By taking on the upfront work of helping others, you are ensuring project success at all costs.

Now that you're up and running, and your people are too, let's take a brief interlude into monitoring project momentum and motivation.

Monitor Project Momentum & Motivation

Your plans are built, your people are secured, your team is invested and meeting, and now we have to keep your project moving! You clearly have other parts of your job aside from this particular project—or 15 projects!—and this interlude is about remaining focused and motivated on the project outcomes.

It can be very easy to fall into the trap of just executing the Project Plan once you have done all the work of writing it, securing support, and moving along in your day-to-day work life. But we also need to set checkpoints to see if we are actually achieving our desired outcomes.

Should you begin sharing Project Progress with others?

YES! We recommend asking interested parties (often managers, or other project sponsors) how they want to stay in the loop and why. It can be helpful to provide options like:

- ❑ I could update you during our weekly check-in.

- ❑ I could cc: you on written communications to various parties.

- ❑ I could send you a written update.

The Weekly Project Review, from the previous chapter, can help us reflect weekly on project progress. In some cases, you may want to set incremental goals to see if you are on track to meeting your goals. For example, Kelly may want to step back and ask questions like:

- Are we on track to hiring enough tutors?
- How well did our training achieve the desired outcomes?
- How many students are enrolled in the tutoring program?
- Are students in the tutoring program progressing academically?

Different people will care about different aspects of your project. Your manager may value data about student enrollment but another colleague wants to know more about the mood on training day. Never assume your manager or project sponsor even knows what they want to know; the responsibility is on us as Project Managers to figure this out! Try doing the heavy lifting for them by identifying options and asking them to "check the box." It's better than being asked questions later!

	CHAPTER OBJECTIVES	TOGETHER TOOL
1. **Prime the Project**	• Ask yourself useful Project Pre-Work Questions • Draft a Project Statement to align with your Participants • Write a Project Summary to finalize the project	✔ Project Statement ✔ Project Summary
2. **Create Clear Project Roles & Responsibilities**	• Get clear about the actual project work that needs to be done • Figure out who is best positioned to take on which tasks • Determine how to communicate about the project work with your Participants	✔ Clear Roles and Responsibilities ✔ Project Job Description
3. **Plan the Project**	• Determine which Project Planning tool is most effective for you • Decide which Project Columns are necessary for your project • Create Project Buckets to begin chronological project thinking • Break down Project Buckets into Project Tasks	✔ Project Plan
4. **Launch the Project**	• Differentiate your project communication for various Project Stakeholders • Determine your method for launching your project into the world	✔ Project Communications Chart ✔ Project Launch Agenda ✔ Project Launch Emails
5. **Manage Yourself & Others**	• Conduct a Weekly Project Review to keep tasks and the Project Team on track • Create and protect time to do your own Project Work • Design and implement Project Meetings and various forms of communication	✔ Weekly Project Reviews ✔ Project Meeting Agendas
6. **Close & Codify the Project**	• Gather ongoing data to help inform outcomes • Facilitate a Project Debrief to consider successes and challenges • Codify learnings for the future	✔ Formal and Informal Project Feedback ✔ Project Debrief ✔ Project Codification Plan

6

CLOSE AND CODIFY THE PROJECT— and Don't Forget to Celebrate!

In this chapter, you will:
- Gather ongoing data to help inform outcomes
- Facilitate a Project Debrief to consider successes and challenges
- Codify learnings for the future

It can be easy to gather ideas throughout the project and let them fall to the wayside amidst the business of day-to-day work. We want to set up a system to guarantee that we--and our project team members--are collecting feedback along the way! This is important because we will look to the future and apply our lessons learned over time.

CAPTURE ONGOING PROJECT INPUT

Based on capturing anecdotal data and observations, you will likely have many ongoing project adjustments, ideas, and changes for the immediate—and right now! There are multiple methods to collect those thoughts—from formal Stakeholder Surveys to jotting our own notes when observing on site. Let's explore formal methods first.

GATHER FORMAL PROJECT FEEDBACK

Kelly's Tutoring Program

There are a few ways Kelly wants to gather feedback about her tutoring program:

1. Measure actual student outcomes and share them regularly
2. Survey tutors (once mid-program and once at the end) to assess how well they feel supported
3. Conduct a similar survey of the operations teams about their needs
4. Observe the program in action multiple times and take detailed notes (Hint: Build time into calendar now!). This can help Kelly make tweaks along the way and capture ideas for adjustment in the future.

Let's peek at a survey Kelly shared with the district's principals to gather feedback.

Saturday Tutoring Program - Mid-Program Survey

cspader@gmail.com (not shared) Switch account

Please indicate the extent to which you agree with the following statement: Overall, the Saturday Tutoring Program is supporting students to meet their academic growth goals:

○ Strongly agree

○ Agree

○ Neither agree nor disagree

○ Disagree

○ Strongly disagree

Optional - please explain your response to the above.

Your answer

What one change could we make that would most improve program's support of students?

Your answer

Please indicate the extent to which you agree with the following statement: Overall, logistics for the Saturday Tutoring Program have been smooth and efficient:

○ Strongly agree

○ Agree

○ Neither agree nor disagree

○ Disagree

○ Strongly disagree

Optional - please explain your response to the above.

Your answer

What one change could we make that would most improve the smoothness and efficiency of the Saturday Tutoring Program's logistics?

Your answer

Submit   Clear form

6.1 Kelly's Tutoring Program Mid-Semester Survey

As you can see, Kelly picked a combination of multiple choice and open-ended questions, kept it short and sweet, and focused on the actual outcome of student achievement.

You will also want a method to gather informal feedback from your team—and your own observations—along the way.

GATHER INFORMAL PROJECT FEEDBACK

When you are in the midst of a project, you learn a lot along the way. You might notice thoughts like, "Oh my goodness, we HAVE to do XYZ idea next time!" But then off you go running to the next meeting or problem to be solved, and the good idea fades into a void. We need a way to capture real-time project thoughts. Here are a few tricks to give them a place to land for good, and if the project is replicable, use them in the future:

- **Keep a Thought Catcher:** A personal spot to capture Project thoughts in the moment. For more detail, see _The Together Leader_ or _The Together Teacher_ or pop over to the sidebar for a full definition.

- **Make notes in your Plan:** Use the Notes column of your Project Plan or create a second tab to help capture learnings during Project Meetings. Bonus points for this method because your great ideas will be easy to find in the future.

- **Create a Slack channel, email address, or shared Doc:** This will allow Participants to share feedback and questions throughout the project. This method is helpful if you're working with many contributors, especially if they're not part of regular Project Meetings. Just remember to make time on your meeting agenda to review!

- **Issue a formal survey about the project and outcome:** For projects with multiple helpers and stakeholders, you may want to issue a one-time survey that captures their specific feedback on the parts of the project in which they were involved. This is a good option if you are working with someone very senior and you want their input reflected, but don't want to waste their time with a meeting.

If your project is incredibly complex, involves multiple people and has a very discrete endpoint, your project may also warrant a formal debrief. As always, pick and choose the ideas here that align most with your project needs and organizational culture, and tuck the rest away! Should you decide to host a debrief, here's how.

> ## Thought Catchers
> Yes, you heard that right. <u>A place to record topics and ideas for people, projects, or even fun personal stuff</u>. For Together Project Managers, you may want to keep a place in your own personal organization system to record thoughts as you reflect on Project Meetings, site or field visits, or even just ways to improve in the future. Trust me, it will be great to have these ongoing notes in one place as you head into formally debriefing your Project.

> **How will you capture formal AND informal input along the way?** Put these Project Tasks right into your Project Plan now—if you haven't already! And block time in your calendar to review feedback!

Project Debrief: A set-aside time at the end of a project to celebrate, capture learnings, and note improvements for the next time you tackle the same project or something similar.

HOST A PROJECT DEBRIEF

Kelly's Tutoring Program

Let's look at Kelly's Project Debrief Agenda and how she'll approach it with her team. In advance of the meeting, she's asked her people to send reflections on successes and challenges, review key pieces of data, and make choices about what they'd maintain, tweak, or overhaul in the future.

Kelly asks herself:

- Do I actually need a meeting? When is the ideal time to host? Do we need multiple iterations of the same session?
- Who should attend the meeting?
- Should we be in person or on a video or audio call?
- Does the meeting require pre-work? How could this help? How far in advance do I need to communicate?
- How can we celebrate our project outcomes and impact?
- Do any decisions remain? If so, how can we get these made now so they're ready for next project?

Next, Kelly creates a simple agenda to support answering these questions.

Kelly asked her Project Team to complete pre-work before the debrief meeting.

How important is it to build in celebration?

VERY!!! People give our projects their all! Many of our Project Participants are working hard behind the scenes and don't always get to see the impact of their immediate work. Building in celebration—both at the end and along the way—gives people a window into the impact of their work.

PROJECT MANAGER | DEBRIEF MEETING AGENDA

Project Name: Saturday Tutoring Program

Project Debrief Agenda Overview

- *Pre-work: Reflection*
- [10 min] Welcome
- [10 min] Celebrate successes
- [10 min] Pre-work review
- [15 min] Group discussion questions
- [10 min] Project closeout & next steps
- [5 min] Gratitude

Pre-Work: Reflection

Before the Project Debrief, please:

- Review the <u>Saturday Tutoring Program Data Summary</u>.
- Add at last one success and one challenge to the chart below.

Workstreams or Phases	Successes	Challenges
Overall	• Summative evals show that students moved an average of .78 grade levels in math and .6 in reading through the program – illustrating that tutoring was the extra support students needed to get back on-track • 90% of families strongly agree or agree that the program was well-executed and an effective use of students' time • We have built a strong and collaborative project team	
Principal Communication & Engagement	We had more interest from school leaders than expected! Principals were invested and championed our program with families	
Budget	We have spent 95% of our budget	Curriculum was more expensive than budgeted, but we were able to reallocate from the training budget

6.2 Project Debrief Agenda

Close & Codify the Project

The purpose of the pre-work is to gather everyone's voices in advance and prepare to share successes and challenges. If we just ask for people's feedback in the moment, there is a chance we won't hear from everyone or some people's ideas may dominate the conversation. By doing this prior to the meeting, the project team arrives already aligned on both what to celebrate and adjust for the future.

The sign of a successful project debrief is a rich discussion that yields thoughtful next steps! Let's look at Kelly's notes in more detail.

Here's how Kelly made sure her tutoring project was set up for future success:

- **Celebrated the project success**—and even brought cupcakes!
- **Gave time for everyone to review** each other's pre-work and add comments
- **Created space for deep discussion** to explore other people's thoughts and expand upon them
- **Captured team feedback and identified concrete levels of change**, using the language "sustain, tweak, overhaul"

The final step in your Project Debrief will be to codify future learnings, and figure out where to store them and how to transfer the knowledge to those who'll need it moving forward.

> **If needed, take a minute to get your Project Debrief Meeting scheduled and your agenda drafted.** Sketch your own Debrief now—and feel free to use our template at <u>thetogetherpress.com/the-together-project-manager</u> to get a head start.

Project Name: _____

Project Debrief Agenda Overview

- *Pre-work: Reflection*
- [10 min] Welcome
- [10 min] Celebrate successes
- [10 min] Pre-work review
- [15 min] Group discussion questions
- [10 min] Project closeout & next steps
- [5 min] Gratitude

Pre-Work: Reflection

Before the Project Debrief, please:
- Review _____
- Add at last one success and one challenge to the chart below.

Workstreams or Phases	Successes	Challenges
Overall		
Workstream / Phase 1		
Workstream / Phase 2		

6.3 Project Debrief Agenda Template

CODIFY FUTURE LEARNINGS

No doubt you've been handed projects in the past with "Go look on Google Drive" kind of directives. I know I have. To avoid inflicting similar pain and confusion on our colleagues, let's make sure we codify clearly.

- **Create a Cover Sheet.** Draft a letter of welcome and explanation for the future Project Manager.

- **Make an Index.** List all pertinent documents related to your project and the order in which to read them.

- **Create tech-easy Back-Ups.** (e.g. Dropbox link, Google Drive file, or Microsoft Teams channel.)

Let's get a glimpse into how Kelly organized her project notes.

**Saturday Tutoring Program Archive—
Cover Letter & Table of Contents**

Hello!

We are excited that you are leading this year's Saturday Tutoring Program. We have a lot to celebrate from our first year, and we are looking forward to seeing this program continue to grow.

My name is Kelly, and I led the project team for the first year of the program. In this archive, our team has pulled together several resources that you can use as a launching place in planning and executing this year's program.

I'd recommend starting with the Project Statement, Project Summary, and the Project Debrief notes to get a sense of what we set out to do and how it went. Then, explore the rest of the files we've archived in this Google Drive folder.

We have seen this program have significant impact on student learning (check out the data summary!), and we are invested in its continued success. Please don't hesitate to reach out to us with questions!

Best,

- Kelly, Assistant Director of Student Support—Project Lead
- Frank, Managing Director of Student Support—Project Sponsor
- Helen, Facilities Director
- Pablo, Assistant Director of Teaching and Learning
- Tonya, Manager of Student Support Finances
- Dante, Assistant Director of Data and Analytics

Archive Table of Contents

Note: We've hyperlinked each file here, but if you're navigating the *Googlea Drive* folder, know that each file name starts with the number & letter on this list, e.g. "1A Project Plan"

1. General
   A. <u>Project Statement</u>
   B. <u>Project Summary</u>
   C. <u>Project plan</u>
   D. <u>Roles & Responsibilities</u>
   E. <u>Project team job descriptions</u>

2. Principal Communication & Engagement
   A. <u>August 21 kick-off deck</u>
   B. <u>Sample email blast blurbs</u>

3. Budget
   A. <u>Budget to actual tracker</u>

4. Facilities
   A. <u>Facilities plan</u>

5. Curriculum
   A. <u>Decision chart & notes aboutother considered vendors</u>

6. Student Recruitment
   A. <u>Priority recruitment list tracker</u>
   B. <u>Virtual info session deck</u>
   C. <u>Newsletter blurb samples</u>

7. Tutor Hiring
   A. <u>Job description</u>
   B. <u>Recruitment blurbs</u>
   C. <u>Interview schedule</u>
   D. <u>Interview materials</u>
   E. <u>Offer letter template</u>

8. Tutor Training
   A. <u>Scope & sequence</u>
   B. <u>Training decks</u>
   C. <u>Feedback survey results</u>

9. Logistical Execution & Course-Correction
   A. <u>Student roster</u>
   B. <u>Schedule</u>
   C. <u>"Lessons learned" tracker</u>

10. Evaluation
    A. <u>Data summary</u>
    B. <u>Student / Parent / Teacher / Tutor / Principal survey results</u>
    C. <u>Project debrief notes</u>

6.4 Kelly's Cover Letter

Yes, this will take a tiny bit of time, but it will yield better results in the future for others. Ultimately, we want your project to carry on without you! We want you to hand it off to another Together Project Manager who can easily run with it and make it stronger without having to start from scratch!

How will you codify your Project Learnings and keep them organized for a future Project Manager?

BUT NOT GOODBYE!

Well, that was a Together Project Manager journey, wasn't it? Whatever your role, we hope that walking through this project process from start to finish will help you invest your stakeholders, communicate clearly, and cross the finish line with finesse. We want people jump at the chance to work on your projects because you communicate so clearly, set others up for success, and connect the project to your organization's mission.

Whether you are brand new to project management or a seasoned project professional, do keep in mind the following as you dive into your projects:

- **Select the simplest approach possible per project.** Please, please don't apply all of these tools to every single project. You will exhaust yourself and those around you. Consider each project carefully and don't be afraid of the quick and dirty Project Plan. Some projects warrant tons of details, filters, cells and all the things, and some, well, some just don't. Also, don't be afraid to apply your Together Project Manager skills to your personal life as well.

- **Stay connected to the mission and what matters.** Most likely, you initially selected this book because you are engaged in some kind of mission-driven work, or maybe you heard about Togetherness from a trusted colleague. Whatever your project may be, stay rooted in the goals and what matters. Celebrate the outcomes and show examples of how your project makes the world a better place.

- **The more planned you are, the more flexible you can be.**

We do not believe plans are meant to be written and then just followed. Rather, I want you to carefully think through every detail, anticipate decisions and forecast thoughtfully SO we can react well when the proverbial rain comes down. Every project has its own set of pitfalls—some of which can be anticipated, many of which cannot—and my hope is that your Project Brain is free and clear, such that you can handle a crisis with grace.

A reminder that you can locate modifiable versions of all Together Templates over at thetogetherpress.com/the-together-project-manager. Take them, make them your own, and share them with us on social media. Add a tag that says **#togetherprojectmanager** so we can take a peek!

 **Instagram:**
@together_teacher

 **Facebook:**
facebook.com/thetogetherteacher

Resource: Glossary

Project Statement: A one-page summary, often including snazzy visuals, that articulates the purpose, participants, and timeline of your project.

Project Summary: A 1–2 page overview of your project, outlining the intended outcomes, key deadlines, roles and responsibilities, and budget for your project.

Project Plan: Articulates the goals, tasks, owners, and resources to accomplish the outcomes of a particular project. It clearly defines all work related to the project and who is in charge of various project pieces.

Project Bucket: The larger categories of a project that have smaller tasks underneath it.

Project Tasks: The steps that make your project run smoothly.

Project Team: The people directly responsible for working on the project tasks with you.

Project Stakeholders: The people impacted by your project.

Project Communications Chart: Identifies your Project Stakeholders (these are different people than your Project Participants who are actually DOING the work), considers how to approach them and plans for ongoing communications.

Project Reviews: A set aside time and process to review your Projects.

Project Debrief: A set-aside time at the end of a project to celebrate, capture learnings, and note improvements for the next time you tackle the same project or something similar.

MOCHA:

M: Manager	Assigns responsibility and holds owner accountable. Makes suggestions, asks questions, and reviews progress.
O: Owner	Overall responsibility for success of the project. Ensures all work is completed.
C: Consulted	Asked for input or needs to be brought into the project.
H: Helper	School-based operations person, district Human Resourcesfor interviews.
A: Approver	Signs off on decisions before finalization.

From The Management Center

RACI:

	Definition	Number of Team Members to Assign
Responsible	Does the work to complete the task	At least 1 per task
Accountable	Delegates work and is the last one to review the task or deliverable before it's deemed complete	Limit to 1 per task
Consulted	Provides input based on either how it will impact their future project work or their domain of expertise on the deliverable itself	No max or minimum
Informed	Needs to be kept in the loop on project progress, rather than roped into the details of every deliverable	No max or minimum

Developed by Kristoffer V. Grude, Tor Haug and Erling S. Andersen

Recommender vs. Decider:

Recommender	Decider
• "Packages" a single recommendation for the Decider • Sets the recommendation, decision, revision, and finalization timeline at the beginning of the project and communicates to all Stakeholders • Faithfully and accurately gathers input from all stated Input groups (but may make decisions regarding entire cohort or representative cohort)	• Schedules time to thoughtfully participate in the decision-making process • Plans and (to the extent possible) adheres to the pre-planned process • Provides clear rationale for any decisions that go against the recommendation and offers support to the Recommender when communicating with Stakeholders

Used with permission from KIPP Texas Public Schools

Resource: Together Tearaway
(next page)

Well, it is not an actual Tearaway (though if you are reading this in hard copy, you are welcome to rip this page out!) But for those of you who reach for this book each time you begin a project—and we hope you will—we thought a little cheat sheet of sorts could be helpful.

	CHAPTER OBJECTIVES	**TOGETHER TOOL**
1. **Prime the Project**	• Ask yourself useful Project Pre-Work Questions • Draft a Project Statement to align with your Participants • Write a Project Summary to finalize the project	✔ Project Statement ✔ Project Summary
2. **Create Clear Project Roles & Responsibilities**	• Get clear about the actual project work that needs to be done • Figure out who is best positioned to take on which tasks • Determine how to communicate about the project work with your Participants	✔ Clear Roles and Responsibilities ✔ Project Job Description
3. **Plan the Project**	• Determine which Project Planning tool is most effective for you • Decide which Project Columns are necessary for your project • Create Project Buckets to begin chronological project thinking • Break down Project Buckets into Project Tasks	✔ Project Plan
4. **Launch the Project**	• Differentiate your project communication for various Project Stakeholders • Determine your method for launching your project into the world	✔ Project Communications Chart ✔ Project Launch Agenda ✔ Project Launch Emails
5. **Manage Yourself & Others**	• Conduct a Weekly Project Review to keep tasks and the Project Team on track • Create and protect time to do your own Project Work • Design and implement Project Meetings and various forms of communication	✔ Weekly Project Reviews ✔ Project Meeting Agendas
6. **Close & Codify the Project**	• Gather ongoing data to help inform outcomes • Facilitate a Project Debrief to consider successes and challenges • Codify learnings for the future	✔ Formal and Informal Project Feedback ✔ Project Debrief ✔ Project Codification Plan

Thank You, Farewell, and We Can Do This

This book is a bit of a departure from our other three publications in that we created one example for you to follow through the entire book—Kelly and her tutoring program. It was inspired by some work we have done with large school districts in the past, and we thought it was complex enough to offer many options to learn from. As always, writing as an extrovert comes with many people to thank.

Maggie, your project management skills are extraordinaire as we birthed this book. To believe you did so while raising two young kids, starting graduate school and supporting your family is miraculous. Also, your motivational texts are everything.

Marin, my eternal forever first and last reader. This is our fourth book with you as my editor, my voice, and our tone. You are the only person we would change an entire timeline to get you this text before you made a break for the Canadian border.

Kendra, your work behind-the-scenes on all things branding, templates, and ensuring our teaching is of the highest quality is Top Notch Together. Your attention to detail is unparalleled and your kid planning skills are second to none!

Emily, I've wanted to work on a project with you since I met you at 2 AM in Vegas after a very delayed flight. I'm so glad we kept in touch, and I'm honored that you spent so much time brainstorming structure, creating exemplars, and adding your overall critical eye to every part of this book.

Chad and Manuel, we did it again. Thank you for being such a creative duo, making sure our books are easy to read, resources are on our websites, and for offering your design eye on everything The Together Group puts out there.

Keith, Ada, Reed, Harriet, and Neala, I appreciate your patience when I'm writing during evenings and weekends, your support during the tricky parts. Thanks for being a huge giant Big Blended Four Kid Four Cat Family. Together Household is on our horizon!

Author Backgrounds

MAIA HEYCK-MERLIN

Maia Heyck-Merlin is the CEO and founder of The Together Group, a very small organization laser-focused on supporting teachers, principals, and school district staff on planning ahead and getting organized. In 2011, she wrote the first edition of the *Together Teacher: Plan Ahead, Get Organized, and Save Time*, and five years later she followed with *The Together Leader: Get Organized for your Success—and Sanity!* Most recently, she founded The Together Press and released *The Together Work-From-Home Teacher* to meet the unique and sudden needs of teachers across the country abruptly going remote during the COVID-19 pandemic.

Formerly, Maia was an upper elementary school teacher, served in multiple leadership roles at Teach For America, and then founded and led the first-ever talent team for Achievement First. She holds a B.A. in Child Development from Tufts University, and is a proud graduate of rural public schools in Central Maine.

Maia lives in the Washington, DC, area with her Four-Kid-Four-Cat-Big-Blended-Family. In her free time, she enjoys her life as an amateur triathlete, Girl Scout troop leader, and neighborhood project planner for block parties and vacations.

EMILY M. REYNOLDS

Emily Reynolds has supported educators through roles in project management, talent strategy, event operations. Currently she works for the Texas Education Agency as a Performance Manager; in this role, she supports agency initiatives in implementing strong project and performance management practices. She began officially working with The Together Group as an independent consultant in 2020, although she had been a long-time Together fan. Prior to consulting, Emily worked for the KIPP Foundation, where she supported local talent leaders across KIPP's network of public charter schools.

Emily holds B.A. degrees in English Literature, History, and Psychology and a Masters of Nonprofit Studies from Arizona State University. She lives in Phoenix where she enjoys long walks with her husband and miniature dachshund, playing boardgames, and trying to keep up with a too-long list of books to read.

The
Together
Press™

thetogetherpress.com

A powerful and practical book for PROJECT MANAGERS!

Maia Heyck-Merlin's newest book takes readers through each stage of the project planning process:

- *Prime the Project*
- *Create Clear Project Roles & Responsibilities*
- *Plan the Project*
- *Launch the Project*
- *Manage Yourself & Others*
- *Close & Codify the Project*

Maia takes readers on a deep dive into the entire cycle of project management from start to finish. In each chapter, you'll find concrete examples, modifiable templates, FAQs, definitions, and Reader Reflections to help you think deeply about your project.

At the end of this book, you should be able to say, "I'm the kind of Together Project Manager who plans in advance, practices flexibility when things change, invests people in the purpose, supports my team in getting the work done, communicates strategically, and celebrates completion."

The Together Press™

thetogetherpress.com

Made in the USA
Middletown, DE
21 April 2022

64553561R10075